The Poetry of Abu'l-Ala Al-Maarri

Abul 'Ala Al-Ma'arri was born in December 973 in modern day Maarrat al-Nu'man, near Aleppo, in Syria.

He was a member of the Banu Sulayman, a noted family of Ma'arra, belonging to the larger Tanukh tribe that had formed part of the aristocracy in Syria dating back many hundreds of years.

Aged only four he was rendered virtually blind due to smallpox and whilst this was thought to explain his pessimistic outlook on life and his fellow man it seems too young an age to support that.

He was educated at Aleppo, Tripoli and Antioch and the area itself was part of the Abbasid Caliphate, the third Islamic caliphate, during what is now considered the Golden Age of Islam.

During his schooling he began to write poetry, perhaps from as young as 11 or 12.

In 1004-5 Al-Ma'arri learned that his father had died and, in commemoration, wrote an elegy in praise. A few years later, as an established poet and with a desire to see more of life and culture in Baghdad, he journeyed there, staying for perhaps as long as eighteen months. However, although he was respected and well received in literary circles he found the experience at odds with his growing ascetic beliefs and resisted all efforts to purchase his works. He was also by now a somewhat controversial figure and although on the whole respected his views on religion were now also causing him trouble.

By 1010 with news of his mother ailing back at home he started the journey back to Ma'rra but arrived shortly after her death.

He would now remain in Ma'arra for the rest of his life, continuing with his self-imposed ascetic style, refusing to sell his poems, living alone in seclusion and adhering to a strict vegetarian diet. Though he was confined, he lived out his years continuing his work and collaborating with others and enjoyed great respect despite some of the controversy associated with his beliefs.

He is often now described as a "pessimistic freethinker". He attacked the dogmas of organised religion and rejected Islam and other faiths. Intriguingly Al-Ma'arri held anti-natalist views; children should not be born to spare them the pains of life.

One of the recurring themes of his philosophy was the truth of reason against competing claims of custom, tradition, and authority. Al-Ma'arri taught that religion was a "fable invented by the ancients", worthless except to those who exploit the credulous masses. He went on to explain "Do not suppose the statements of the prophets to be true; they are all fabrications. Men lived comfortably till they came and spoiled life. The sacred books are only such a set of idle tales as any age could have and indeed did actually produce.

However, Al-Ma'arri was still a monotheist, but believed that God was impersonal and that the afterlife did not exist. For someone who was not widely travelled Al-Ma'arri stated that monks in their cloisters or devotees in their mosques were blindly following the beliefs of their locality: if they were born among Magians or Sabians they would have become Magians or Sabians, further declaring, rather boldly, that

"The inhabitants of the earth are of two sorts: those with brains, but no religion, and those with religion, but no brains."

Abul 'Ala Al-Ma'arri never married and died aged 83, in May 1057 in his hometown, Maarrat al-Nu'man.

Even on Al-Ma'arri's epitaph, he wanted it written that his life was a wrong done by his father and not one committed by himself.

Today, despite fundamentalists and jihadists at odds with his thinking and viewing him as a heretic, Al-Ma'arri is regarded as one of the greatest of classical Arabic poets as these translated work readily attest too.

Index of Contents

TO HIS ROYAL HIGHNESS EMIR FEISAL IN WHOM ARE CENTRED THE HOPES AND ASPIRATIONS OF THE SYRIAN PEOPLE FOR A UNITED SYRIA THIS BOOK IS DEDICATED

"His poems generally known as the Luzumiyat arrest attention by their boldness and originality as well as by the sombre and earnest tone which pervades them."
Raynold A. Nicholson: A History of the Arabs.

"Abu'l-Ala is a poet many centuries ahead of his time."
Von Kremer.

TO ABU'L-ALA by Ameen Rihani

In thy fountained peristyles of Reason
Glows the light and flame of desert noons;
And in the cloister of thy pensive Fancy
Wisdom burns the spikenard of her moons.

Closed by Fate the portals of the dwelling
Of thy sight, the light thus inward flowed;
And on the shoulders of the crouching Darkness

Thou hast risen to the highest road.

I have seen thee walking with Canopus
Through the stellar spaces of the night;
I have heard thee asking thy Companion,
"Where be now my staff, and where thy light?"

Abu'l-Ala, in the heaving darkness,
Didst thou not the whisperings hear of me?
In thy star-lit wilderness, my Brother,
Didst thou not a burdened shadow see?

I have walked and I have slept beside thee,
I have laughed and I have wept as well;
I have heard the voices of thy silence
Melting in thy Jannat and thy hell.

I remember, too, that once the Saki
Filled the antique cup and gave it thee;
Now, filled with the treasures of thy wisdom,
Thou dost pass that very cup to me.

By the God of thee, my Syrian Brother,
Which is best, the Saki's cup or thine?
Which the mystery divine uncovers—
If the cover covers aught divine.

And if it lies hid in the soul of silence
Like incense in the dust of ambergris,
Wouldst thou burn it to perfume the terror
Of the caverns of the dried-up seas?

Where'er it be, Oh! let it be, my Brother.—
Though "thrice-imprisoned,"[9] thou hast forged us more
Solid weapons for the life-long battle
Than all the Heaven-taught Armorers of yore.

"Thrice-imprisoned," thou wert e'en as mighty,
In the boundless kingdom of the mind,
As the whirlwind that compels the ocean,
As the thunder that compels the wind.

"Thrice-imprisoned," thou wert freer truly
Than the liegeless Arab on his mare,—
Freer than the bearers of the sceptre,—
Freer than the winged lords of the air.

"Thrice-imprisoned," thou hast sung of freedom

As but a few of all her heroes can;
Thou hast undermined the triple prison
Of the mind and heart and soul of man.

In thy fountained peristyles of Reason
Glows the light and flame of desert noons;
And in the cloister of thy pensive Fancy
Wisdom burns the spikenard of her moons.

PREFACE

When Christendom was groping amid the superstitions of the Dark Ages, and the Norsemen were ravaging the western part of Europe, and the princes of Islam were cutting each other's throats in the name of Allah and his Prophet, Abu'l-Ala'l-Ma'arri was waging his bloodless war against the follies and evils of his age. He attacked the superstitions and false traditions of law and religion, proclaiming the supremacy of the mind; he hurled his trenchant invectives at the tyranny, the bigotry, and the quackery of his times, asserting the supremacy of the soul; he held the standard of reason high above that of authority, fighting to the end the battle of the human intellect. An intransigeant with the exquisite mind of a sage and scholar, his weapons were never idle. But he was, above all, a poet; for when he stood before the eternal mystery of Life and Death, he sheathed his sword and murmured a prayer.

Abu'l-Ala'l-Ma'arri, [1] the Lucretius of Islam, the Voltaire of the East, was born in the spring of the year 973 A.D., in the obscure village of Ma'arrah, [2] which is about eighteen hours' journey south of Halab (Aleppo). And instead of Ahmad ibn Abdallah ibn Sulaiman ut-Tanukhi (of the tribe of Tanukh), he was called Abu'l-Ala (the Father of the Sublime), by which patronymic of distinction he is popularly known throughout the Arabic speaking world.

When a boy, Abu'l-Ala was instructed by his father; and subsequently he was sent to Halab, where he pursued his studies under the tutelage of the grammarian Muhammad ibn Abdallah ibn us-Sad. His literary proclivity was evinced in his boyhood, and he wrote verse, we are told, before he was ten. Of these juvenile pieces, however, nothing was preserved.

He was about five years old when he fell a victim to small-pox and almost lost his sight from it. But a weakness in his eyes continued to trouble him and he became, in middle age, I presume, totally blind. [3] Some of his biographers would have us believe he was born blind; others state that he completely lost his sight when he was attacked by the virulent disease; and a few intimate that he could see slightly at least with the right eye. As to whether or not he was blind when he was sent to Halab to pursue his studies, his biographers do not agree. My theory, based on the careful perusal of his poems and on a statement advanced by one of his biographers, [4] is that he lost his sight gradually, and total blindness must have come upon him either in his youth or his middle age. [5] Were we to believe that he was born blind or that he suffered the complete loss of his sight in his boyhood, we should be at a loss to know, not how he wrote his books, for that was done by dictation; not how he taught his pupils, for that was done by lectures; but how he himself was taught in the absence in those days of a regular system of instruction for the blind.

In 1010 A.D. he visited Baghdad, the centre of learning and intelligence and the capital of the Abbaside Khalifs, where he passed about two years and became acquainted with most of the literary men of the age. [6] He attended the lectures and the readings of the leading doctors and grammarians, meeting with a civil reception at the hand of most of them.

He also journeyed to Tripoli, [7] which boasted, in those days, of many public libraries; and, stopping at Ladhekiyah, he lodged in a monastery where he met and befriended a very learned monk. They discussed theology and metaphysics, digressing now and then into the profane. Indeed, the skepticism which permeates Abu'l-Ala's writings must have been nursed in that convent by both the monk and the poet.

These are virtually the only data extant showing the various sources of Abu'l-Ala's learning; but to one endowed with a keen perception, a powerful intellect, a prodigious memory, together with strong innate literary predilections, they seem sufficient. He was especially noted for the extraordinary memory he possessed; and around this our Arab biographers and historians weave a thick net of anecdotes, or rather fables. I have no doubt that one with such a prodigious memory could retain in a few minutes what the average person could not; but when we are told that Abu'l-Ala once heard one of his pupils speaking with a friend in a foreign tongue, and repeated there and then the long conversation, word for word, without having the slightest idea of its meaning, we are disposed to be skeptical. Many such anecdotes are recorded and quoted by his Arab biographers without as much as intimating a single doubt. [8] The fact that he was blind partly explains the abnormal development of his memory.

His career as poet and scholar dates from the time he returned from Baghdad. This, so far as is known, was the last journey he made; and his home became henceforth his earthly prison. He calls himself "A double-fettered Captive," [9] his solitude being the one and his blindness the other. Like most of the scholars of his age, in the absence of regular educational institutions, with perhaps one or two exceptions, he had to devote a part of his time to the large number of pupils that flocked to Ma'arrah from all parts of Asia Minor, Arabia, and India. Aside from this, he dictated to his numerous amanuenses on every possible and known subject. He is not only a poet of the first rank, but an essayist, a literary critic, and a mathematician as well. Everything he wrote was transcribed by many of his admirers, as was the fashion then, and thus circulated far and near. Nothing, however, was preserved but his Diwans, his Letters and the Epistle of Forgiveness, [10] of which I shall yet have occasion to speak. [11]

His reputation as poet and scholar had now, after his return from Baghdad, overleaped the horizons, as one writer has it. Honors were conferred upon him successively by the rulers and the scholars of his age. His many noted admirers were in constant communication with him. He was now looked upon as "the master of the learned, the chief of the wise, and the sole monarch of the bards of his century." Ma'arrah [12] became the Mecca of every literary aspirant; ambitious young scholars came there for enlightenment and inspiration. And Abu'l-Ala, although a pessimist, received them with his wonted kindness and courtesy. He imparted to them what he knew, and told them candidly what he would not teach, since, unlike other philosophers, he was not able to grasp the truth, nor compass the smallest of the mysteries of creation. In his latter days, youthful admirers sought his blessing, which he, as the childless father of all, graciously conferred, but with no self-assumed spiritual or temporal authority.

For thirty years he remained a vegetarian, living the life of an ascetic. [13] This mode of living led his enemies to accuse him of renouncing Islam and embracing Brahminism, one of the tenets of which forbids the slaughter of animals. The accusation was rather sustained by the dispassionate attitude he held towards it, and, furthermore, by his vehement denunciation of the barbarous practice of killing animals for food or for sport.

Most of the censors of Abu'l-Ala were either spurred to their task by bigotry or animated by jealousy and ignorance. They held him up to ridicule and opprobrium, and such epithets as heretic, atheist, renegade, etc., were freely applied. But he was supremely indifferent to them all, [14] and never would he cross swords with any particular individual; he attacked the false doctrines they were teaching, turning a deaf ear to the virulent vituperations they hurled upon him. I fail to find in the three volumes of his poems, even in the Letters, one acrimonious line savoring of personality.

Ibn-Khillikan, The Plutarch of Arabia, who is cautious and guarded in his statements, speaking of Abu'l-Ala, truly says:

"His asceticism, his deep sense of right and wrong, his powerful intellect, his prodigious memory, and his wide range of learning, are alike acknowledged by both friend and foe."

His pessimism was natural, in part hereditary. The man was nothing if not genuine and sincere. Ruthlessly he said what he thought and felt. He had no secrets to hide from the world, no thoughts which he dared not express. His soul was as open as Nature; his mind was the polished mirror of his age. [15] It may be that had he not been blind-stricken and had not small-pox disfigured his features, he might have found a palliative in human society. His pessimism might not have been cured, but it might have been rendered at least enticing. Good-fellowship might have robbed it of its sting. Nor is his strong aversion to marriage, in view of these facts, surprising.

He lived to know that "his fame spread from the sequestered village of Ma'arrah to the utmost confines of the Arabic speaking world." In the spring of 1055 A.D. he died, and was buried in a garden surrounding his home. Adh-Dhahabi states that there were present at his grave eighty poets, and that the Koran was read there two hundred times in a fortnight. Eighty poets in the small town of Ma'arrah sounds incredible. But we must bear in mind that almost every one who studies the Arabic grammar has also to study prosody and versification and thus become at least a rhymster. Even to-day, the death of a noted person among the Arabs, is always an occasion for the display of much eloquence and tears, both in prose and verse.

Abu'l-Ala, beside being a poet and scholar of the first rank, was also one of the foremost thinkers of his age. Very little is said of his teachings, his characteristics, his many-sided intellect, in the biographies I have read. The fact that he was a liberal thinker, a trenchant writer,—free, candid, downright, independent, skeptical withal,—answers for the neglect on the part of Mohammedan doctors, who, when they do discuss him, try to conceal from the world what his poems unquestionably reveal. I am speaking, of course, of the neglect after his death. For during his life-time he was much honored, as I have shown, and many distinguished travellers came especially to Ma'arrah to see him. He was also often called upon to act as intercessor with the Emirs for the natives of his village. [16]

The larger collection of his poems, the Luzumiyat, [17] was published in Cairo, in two volumes, by Azeez Zind, from an original Ms. written in the twelfth century, under Abu'l-Ala's own title Luzum ma la Yalzam, or the Necessity of what is Unnecessary. This title refers to the special system of rhyming which the poet adopted. And the poems, published in desultory fashion, were written, it seems, at different periods of his life, and are arranged according to his particular alphabetical system of rhyming. They bear no titles except, "And he also says, rhyming with so and so," whatever the consonant and vowel may be. In his Preface to the Luzumiyat he says:

"It happened that I composed these poems during the past years, and in them I have always aimed at the truth. They are certainly free from the blandishments of exaggeration. And while some of them are written in glorification of God, who is above such glory, others are, as it were, a reminder to those who forget, a pinch to those who sleep, and a warning to the children of the earth against the wiles of the great world, where human rights and human gratitude are often strangled by the same hand of Fate."

As for the translation of these chosen quatrains, let me say at the outset that it is almost impossible to adhere to the letter thereof and convey the meaning without being insipid, dull, and at times even ridiculous. There being no affinity between the Arabic and the English, their standards of art and beauty widely differ, and in the process of transformation the outer garment at times must necessarily be doffed. I have always adhered to the spirit, however, preserving the native imagery where it was not too clannish or grotesque. I have added nothing that was foreign to the ruling idea, nor have I omitted anything that was necessary to the completion of the general thought. One might get an idea of what is called a scholarly translation from the works of any of the Orientalists who have made a study of Abu'l-Ala. The first English scholar to mention the poet, as far as I know, was J. D. Carlisle, who in his "Specimens of Arabic Poetry", published in 1810, has paraphrased in verse a quatrain on Pride and Virtue. He also translated into Latin one of Abu'l-Ala's bold epigrams, fearing, I suppose, to publish it at that time in English.

The quatrains which are here published are culled from the three Volumes of his poems, and they are arranged, as nearly as may be, in the logical order of their sequence of thought. They form a kind of eclogue, which the poet-philosopher delivers from his prison in Ma'arrah.

Once, in Damascus, I visited, with some friends, a distinguished Sufi; and when the tea was being served, our host held forth on the subject of Abu'l-Ala's creed. He quoted from the Luzumiyat to show that the poet-philosopher of Ma'arrah was a true Sufi, and of the highest order. "In his passionate hatred of the vile world and all the vile material manifestations of life," quoth our host, "he was like a dervish dancing in sheer bewilderment; a holy man, indeed, melting in tears before the distorted image of Divinity. In his aloofness, as in the purity of his spirit, the ecstatic negations of Abu'l-Ala can only be translated in terms of the Sufi's creed. In his raptures, shathat, he was as distant as Ibn ul-Arabi; and in his bewilderment, heirat, he was as deeply intoxicated as Ibn ul-Fared. If others have symbolized the Divinity in wine, he symbolized it in Reason, which is the living oracle of the Soul; he has, in a word, embraced Divinity under the cover of a philosophy of extinction."...

This, and more such from our Sufi host, to which the guests gently nodded understanding. One of them, a young poet and scholar, even added that most of the irreligious opinions that are found in the Luzumiyat were forced upon the poet by the rigorous system of rhyming he adopted. The Rhyme, then, is responsible for the heresies of Abu'l-Ala! Allah be praised! But this view of the matter was not new to me. I have heard it expressed by zealous Muslim scholars, who see in Abu'l-Ala an adversary too strong to be allowed to enlist with the enemy. They will keep him, as one of the "Pillars of the Faith," at any cost. Coming from them, therefore, this rhyme-begotten heresy theory is not surprising.

But I am surprised to find a European scholar like Professor Margoliouth giving countenance to such views; even repeating, to support his own argument, [18] such drivel. For if the system of rhyme-ending imposes upon the poet his irreligious opinions, how can we account for them in his prose writings? How, for instance, explain his book "Al-fusul wal Ghayat" (The Chapters and the Purposes), a work in which he parodied the Koran itself, and which only needed, as he said, to bring it to the standard of the Book, "the polishing of four centuries of reading in the pulpit?" And how account for his "Risalat ul-Ghufran" (Epistle of Forgiveness), a most remarkable work both in form and conception?—a Divina Comedia in its cotyledonous state, as it were, only that Abu'l-Ala does not seem to have relished the idea of visiting Juhannam. He must have felt that in his "three earthly prisons" he had had enough of it. So he visits the Jannat and there meets the pagan bards of Arabia lulling themselves in eternal bliss under the eternal shades of the sidr tree, writing and reading and discussing poetry. Now, to people the Muslem's Paradise with heathen poets who have been forgiven,—hence the title of the Work,—and received among the blest,—is not this clear enough, bold enough, loud enough even for the deaf and the blind? "The idea," says Professor Nicholson, speaking of The Epistle of Forgiveness, [19] "is carried out with such ingenuity and in a spirit of audacious burlesque that reminds one of Lucien."

This does not mean, however, that the work is essentially of a burlesque quality. Abu'l-Ala had humor; but his earnest tone is never so little at an ebb as when he is in his happiest mood. I quote from The Epistle of Forgiveness:

"Sometimes you may find a man skilful in his trade," says the Author, "perfect in sagacity and in the use of arguments, but when he comes to religion he is found obstinate, so does he follow in the old groove. Piety is implanted in human nature; it is deemed a sure refuge. To the growing child, that which falls from his elders' lips is a lesson that abides with him all his life. Monks in their cloisters and devotees in their mosques accept their creed just as a story is handed down from him who tells it, without distinguishing between a true interpreter and a false. If one of these had found his kin among the Magians, or among the Sabians, he would have become nearly or quite like them."

It does seem, too, that the strain of heterodoxy in Abu'l-Ala is partly hereditary. His father, who was also a poet of some distinction, and his maternal uncle, were both noted for their liberal opinions in religious matters. And he himself, alluding in one of his poems to those who reproached him for not making the pilgrimage to Mecca, says that neither his father, nor his cousin, nor his uncle had pilgrimaged at all, and that he will not be denied forgiveness, if they are forgiven. And if they are not, he had as lief share their fate.

But aside from his prose writings, in which, do what we may, we can not explain away his supposed heresies, we find in the Luzumiyat themselves his dominant ideas on religion, for instance, being a superstition; wine, an unmitigated evil; virtue, its own reward; the cremation of the dead, a virtue; the slaughter or even the torture of animals a crime; [20] doubt, a way to truth; reason, the only prophet and guide;—we find these ideas clothed in various images and expressed in varied forms, but unmistakable in whatever guise we find them. Here, for instance, is Professor Nicholson's almost literal translation of a quatrain from the Luzumiyat:

Hanifs [21] are stumbling, Christians gone astray,
Jews wildered, Magians far on error's way:—
We mortals are composed of two great schools,
Enlightened knaves or else religious fools.

And here is the same idea, done in a large picture. The translation, literal too, is mine:

'Tis strange that Kusrah and his people wash
Their faces in the staling of the kine;
And that the Christians say, Almighty God

Was tortured, mocked, and crucified in fine:
And that the Jews should picture Him as one
Who loves the odor of a roasting chine;
And stranger still that Muslems travel far
To kiss a black stone said to be divine:—
Almighty God! will all the human race
Stray blindly from the Truth's most sacred shrine? [22]

The East still remains the battle-ground of the creeds. And the Europeans, though they shook off their fetters of moral and spiritual slavery, would keep us in ours to facilitate the conquests of European commence. Thus the terrible Dragon, which is fed by the foreign missionary and the native priest, by the theologians and the ulama, and which still preys upon the heart and mind of Orient nations, is as active to-day as it was ten centuries ago. Let those consider this, who think Von Kremer exaggerated when he said, "Abu'l-Ala is a poet many centuries ahead of his time."

Before closing, I wish to call attention to a question which, though unimportant in itself, is nevertheless worthy of the consideration of all admirers of Arabic and Persian literature. I refer to the similarity of thought which exists between Omar Khayyam and Abu'l-Ala. The former, I have reason to believe, was an imitator or a disciple of the latter. The birth of the first poet and the death of the second are not very far apart: they both occurred about the middle of the eleventh century. The English reading public here and abroad has already formed its opinion of Khayyam. Let it not, therefore, be supposed that in making this claim I aim to shake or undermine its great faith. My desire is to confirm, not to weaken,—to expand, not contract,—the Oriental influence on the Occidental mind.

Whoever will take the trouble, however, to read Omar Khayyam in conjunction with what is here translated of Abu'l-Ala, can not fail to see the striking similarity in thought and image of certain phases of the creed or the lack of creed of both poets. [23] To be sure, the skepticism and pessimism of Omar are to a great extent imported from Ma'arrah. But the Arab philosopher in his religious opinions is far more outspoken than the Persian tent-maker. I do not say that Omar was a plagiarist; but I say this: just as Voltaire, for instance, acquired most of his liberal and skeptical views from Hobbes, Locke and Bayle, so did Omar acquire his from Abu'l-Ala. In my notes to these quatrains I have quoted in comparison from both the Fitzgerald and the Herron-Allen versions of the Persian poet; and with so much or so little said, I leave the matter in the hands of the reader, who, upon a careful examination, will doubtless bear me out as to this point.

THE LUZUMIYAT OF ABU'L-ALA

I
The sable wings of Night pursuing day
Across the opalescent hills, display
The wondrous star-gems which the fiery suns
Are scattering upon their fiery way.

II
O my Companion, Night is passing fair,

Fairer than aught the dawn and sundown wear;
And fairer, too, than all the gilded days
Of blond Illusion and its golden snare.

III
Hark, in the minarets muazzens call
The evening hour that in the interval
Of darkness Ahmad might remembered be,—
Remembered of the Darkness be they all.

IV
And hear the others who with cymbals try
To stay the feet of every passer-by:
The market-men along the darkling lane
Are crying up their wares.—Oh! let them cry.

V
Mohammed or Messiah! Hear thou me,
The truth entire nor here nor there can be;
How should our God who made the sun and moon
Give all his light to One, I cannot see.

VI
Come, let us with the naked Night now rest
And read in Allah's Book the sonnet best:
The Pleiads—ah, the Moon from them departs,—
She draws her veil and hastens toward the west.

VII
The Pleiads follow; and our Ethiop Queen,
Emerging from behind her starry screen,
Will steep her tresses in the saffron dye
Of dawn, and vanish in the morning sheen.

VIII
The secret of the day and night is in
The constellations, which forever spin
Around each other in the comet-dust;—
The comet-dust and humankind are kin.

IX
But whether of dust or fire or foam, the glaive
Of Allah cleaves the planet and the wave
Of this mysterious Heaven-Sea of life,
And lo! we have the Cradle of the Grave.

X
The Grave and Cradle, the untiring twain,

Who in the markets of this narrow lane
Bordered of darkness, ever give and take
In equal measure—what's the loss or gain?

XI

Ay, like the circles which the sun doth spin
Of gossamer, we end as we begin;
Our feet are on the heads of those that pass,
But ever their Graves around our Cradles grin.

XII

And what avails it then that Man be born
To joy or sorrow?—why rejoice or mourn?
The doling doves are calling to the rose;
The dying rose is bleeding o'er the thorn.

XIII

And he the Messenger, who takes away
The faded garments, purple, white, and gray
Of all our dreams unto the Dyer, will
Bring back new robes to-morrow—so they say.

XIV

But now the funeral is passing by,
And in its trail, beneath this moaning sky,
The howdaj comes,—both vanish into night;
To me are one, the sob, the joyous cry.

XV

With tombs and ruined temples groans the land
In which our forbears in the drifting sand
Arise as dunes upon the track of Time
To mark the cycles of the moving hand

XVI

Of Fate. Alas! and we shall follow soon
Into the night eternal or the noon;
The wayward daughters of the spheres return
Unto the bosom of their sun or moon.

XVII

And from the last days of Thamud and 'Ad
Up to the first of Hashem's fearless lad,
Who smashed the idols of his mighty tribe,
What idols and what heroes Death has had!

XVIII

Tread lightly, for the mighty that have been

Might now be breathing in the dust unseen;
Lightly, the violets beneath thy feet
Spring from the mole of some Arabian queen.

XIX

Many a grave embraces friend and foe
Behind the curtain of this sorry show
Of love and hate inscrutable; alas!
The Fates will always reap the while they sow.

XX

The silken fibre of the fell Zakkum,
As warp and woof, is woven on the loom
Of life into a tapestry of dreams
To decorate the chariot-seat of Doom.

XXI

And still we weave, and still we are content
In slaving for the sovereigns who have spent
The savings of the toiling of the mind
Upon the glory of Dismemberment.

XXII

Nor king nor slave the hungry Days will spare;
Between their fangéd Hours alike we fare:
Anon they bound upon us while we play
Unheeding at the threshold of their Lair.

XXIII

Then Jannat or Juhannam? From the height
Of reason I can see nor fire nor light
That feeds not on the darknesses; we pass
From world to world, like shadows through the night.

XXIV

Or sleep—and shall it be eternal sleep
Somewhither in the bosom of the deep
Infinities of cosmic dust, or here
Where gracile cypresses the vigil keep!

XXV

Upon the threshing-floor of life I burn
Beside the Winnower a word to learn;
And only this: Man's of the soil and sun,
And to the soil and sun he shall return.

XXVI

And like a spider's house or sparrow's nest,

The Sultan's palace, though upon the crest
Of glory's mountain, soon or late must go:
Ay, all abodes to ruin are addrest.

XXVII

So, too, the creeds of Man: the one prevails
Until the other comes; and this one fails
When that one triumphs; ay, the lonesome world
Will always want the latest fairy-tales.

XXVIII

Seek not the Tavern of Belief, my friend,
Until the Sakis there their morals mend;
A lie imbibed a thousand lies will breed,
And thou'lt become a Saki in the end.

XXIX

By fearing whom I trust I find my way
To truth; by trusting wholly I betray
The trust of wisdom; better far is doubt
Which brings the false into the light of day.

XXX

Or wilt thou commerce have with those who make
Rugs of the rainbow, rainbows of the snake,
Snakes of a staff, and other wondrous things?—
The burning thirst a mirage can not slake.

XXXI

Religion is a maiden veiled in prayer,
Whose bridal gifts and dowry those who care
Can buy in Mutakallem's shop of words
But I for such, a dirham can not spare.

XXXII

Why linger here, why turn another page?
Oh! seal with doubt the whole book of the age;
Doubt every one, even him, the seeming slave
Of righteousness, and doubt the canting sage.

XXXIII

Some day the weeping daughters of Hadil
Will say unto the bulbuls: "Let's appeal
To Allah in behalf of Brother Man
Who's at the mercy now of Ababil."

XXXIV

Of Ababil! I would the tale were true,—

Would all the birds were such winged furies too;
The scourging and the purging were a boon
For me, O my dear Brothers, and for you.

XXXV
Methinks Allah divides me to complete
His problem, which with Xs is replete;
For I am free and I am too in chains
Groping along the labyrinthine street.

XXXVI
And round the Well how oft my Soul doth grope
Athirst; but lo! my Bucket hath no Rope:
I cry for water, and the deep, dark Well
Echoes my wailing cry, but not my hope.

XXXVII
Ah, many have I seen of those who fell
While drawing, with a swagger, from the Well;
They came with Rope and Bucket, and they went
Empty of hand another tale to tell.

XXXVIII
The I in me standing upon the brink
Would leap into the Well to get a drink;
But how to rise once in the depth, I cry,
And cowardly behind my logic slink.

XXXIX
And she: "How long must I the burden bear?
How long this tattered garment must I wear?"
And I: "Why wear it? Leave it here, and go
Away without it—little do I care."

XL
But once when we were quarreling, the door
Was opened by a Visitor who bore
Both Rope and Pail; he offered them and said:
"Drink, if you will, but once, and nevermore."

XLI
One draught, more bitter than the Zakkum tree,
Brought us unto the land of mystery
Where rising Sand and Dust and Flame conceal
The door of every Caravanseri.

XLII
We reach a door and there the legend find.

"To all the Pilgrims of the Human Mind:
Knock and pass on!" We knock and knock and knock;
But no one answers save the moaning wind.

XLIII

How like a door the knowledge we attain,
Which door is on the bourne of the Inane;
It opens and our nothingness is closed,—
It closes and in darkness we remain.

XLIV

Hither we come unknowing, hence we go;
Unknowing we are messaged to and fro;
And yet we think we know all things of earth
And sky—the suns and stars we think we know.

XLV

Apply thy wit, O Brother, here and there
Upon this and upon that; but beware
Lest in the end—ah, better at the start
Go to the Tinker for a slight repair.

XLVI

And why so much ado, and wherefore lay
The burden of the years upon the day
Of thy vain dreams? Who polishes his sword
Morning and eve will polish it away.

XLVII

I heard it whispered in the cryptic streets
Where every sage the same dumb shadow meets:
"We are but words fallen from the lipe of Time
Which God, that we might understand, repeats."

XLVIII

Another said: "The creeping worm hath shown,
In her discourse on human flesh and bone,
That Man was once the bed on which she slept—
The walking dust was once a thing of stone."

XLIX

And still another: "We are coins which fade
In circulation, coins which Allah made
To cheat Iblis: the good and bad alike
Are spent by Fate upon a passing shade."

L

And in the pottery the potter cried,

As on his work shone all the master's pride—
"How is it, Rabbi, I, thy slave, can make
Such vessels as nobody dare deride?"

LI
The Earth then spake: "My children silent be;
Same are to God the camel and the flea:
He makes a mess of me to nourish you,
Then makes a mess of you to nourish me."

LII
Now, I believe the Potter will essay
Once more the Wheel, and from a better clay
Will make a better Vessel, and perchance
A masterpiece which will endure for aye.

LIII
With better skill he even will remould
The scattered potsherds of the New and Old;
Then you and I will not disdain to buy,
Though in the mart of Iblis they be sold.

LIV
Sooth I have told the masters of the mart
Of rusty creeds and Babylonian art
Of magic. Now the truth about myself—
Here is the secret of my wincing heart.

LV
I muse, but in my musings I recall
The days of my iniquity; we're all—
An arrow shot across the wilderness,
Somewhither, in the wilderness must fall.

LVI
I laugh, but in my laughter-cup I pour
The tears of scorn and melancholy sore;
I who am shattered by the hand of Doubt,
Like glass to be remoulded nevermore.

LVII
I wheedle, too, even like my slave Zeidun,
Who robs at dawn his brother, and at noon
Prostrates himself in prayer—ah, let us pray
That Night might blot us and our sins, and soon.

LVIII
But in the fatal coils, without intent,

We sin; wherefore a future punishment?
They say the metal dead a deadly steel
Becomes with Allah's knowledge and consent.

LIX

And even the repentant sinner's tear
Falling into Juhannam's very ear,
Goes to its heart, extinguishes its fire
For ever and forever,—so I hear.

LX

Between the white and purple Words of Time
In motley garb with Destiny I rhyme:
The colored glasses to the water give
The colors of a symbolry sublime.

LXI

How oft, when young, my brothers I would shun
If their religious feelings were not spun
Of my own cobweb, which I find was but
A spider's revelation of the sun.

LXII

Now, mosques and churches—even a Kaaba Stone,
Korans and Bibles—even a martyr's bone,—
All these and more my heart can tolerate,
For my religion's love, and love alone.

LXIII

To humankind, O Brother, consecrate
Thy heart, and shun the hundred Sects that prate
About the things they little know about—
Let all receive thy pity, none thy hate.

LXIV

The tavern and the temple also shun,
For sheikh and libertine in sooth are one;
And when the pious knave begins to pule,
The knave in purple breaks his vow anon.

LXV

"The wine's forbidden," say these honest folk,
But for themselves the law they will revoke;
The snivelling sheikh says he's without a garb,
When in the tap-house he had pawned his cloak.

LXVI

Or in the house of lust. The priestly name

And priestly turban once were those of Shame—
And Shame is preaching in the pulpit now—
If pulpits tumble down, I'm not to blame.

LXVII

For after she declaims upon the vows
Of Faith, she pusillanimously bows
Before the Sultan's wine-empurpled throne,
While he and all his courtezans carouse.

LXVIII

Carouse, ye sovereign lords! The wheel will roll
Forever to confound and to console:
Who sips to-day the golden cup will drink
Mayhap to-morrow in a wooden bowl—

LXIX

And silent drink. The tumult of our mirth
Is worse than our mad welcoming of birth:—
The thunder hath a grandeur, but the rains,
Without the thunder, quench the thirst of Earth.

LXX

The Prophets, too, among us come to teach,
Are one with those who from the pulpit preach;
They pray, and slay, and pass away, and yet
Our ills are as the pebbles on the beach.

LXXI

And though around the temple they should run
For seventy times and seven, and in the sun
Of mad devotion drool, their prayers are still
Like their desires of feasting-fancies spun.

LXXII

Oh! let them in the marshes grope, or ride
Their jaded Myths along the mountain-side;
Come up with me, O Brother, to the heights
Where Reason is the prophet and the guide.

LXXIII

"What is thy faith and creed," they ask of me,
"And who art thou? Unseal thy pedigree."—
I am the child of Time, my tribe, mankind,
And now this world's my caravanseri.

LXXIV

Swathe thee in wool, my Sufi friend, and go

Thy way; in cotton I the wiser grow;
But we ourselves are shreds of earth, and soon
The Tailor of the Universe will sew.

LXXV

Ay! suddenly the mystic Hand will seal
The saint's devotion and the sinner's weal;
They worship Saturn, but I worship One
Before whom Saturn and the Heavens kneel.

LXXVI

Among the crumbling ruins of the creeds
The Scout upon his camel played his reeds
And called out to his people,—"Let us hence!
The pasture here is full of noxious weeds."

LXXVII

Among us falsehood is proclaimed aloud,
But truth is whispered to the phantom bowed
Of conscience; ay! and Wrong is ever crowned,
While Right and Reason are denied a shroud.

LXXVIII

And why in this dark Kingdom tribute pay?
With clamant multitudes why stop to pray?
Oh! hear the inner Voice:—"If thou'lt be right,
Do what they deem is wrong, and go thy way."

LXXIX

Thy way unto the Sun the spaces through
Where king Orion's black-eyed huris slew
The Mother of Night to guide the Wings that bear
The flame divine hid in a drop of dew.

LXXX

Hear ye who in the dust of ages creep,
And in the halls of wicked masters sleep:—
Arise! and out of this wan weariness
Where Allah's laughter makes the Devil weep.

LXXXI

Arise! for lo! the Laughter and the Weeping
Reveal the Weapon which the Master's keeping
Above your heads; Oh! take it up and strike!
The lion of tyranny is only sleeping.

LXXXII

Evil and Virtue? Shadows on the street

Of Fate and Vanity,—but shadows meet
When in the gloaming they are hast'ning forth
To drink with Night annihilation sweet.

LXXXIII
And thus the Sun will write and will efface
The mystic symbols which the sages trace
In vain, for all the worlds of God are stored
In his enduring vessels Time and Space.

LXXXIV
For all my learning's but a veil, I guess,
Veiling the phantom of my nothingness;
Howbeit, there are those who think me wise,
And those who think me—even these I bless.

LXXXV
And all my years, as vapid as my lay,
Are bitter morsels of a mystic day,—
The day of Fate, who carries in his lap
December snows and snow-white flowers of May.

LXXXVI
Allah, my sleep is woven through, it seems,
With burning threads of night and golden beams;
But when my dreams are evil they come true;
When they are not, they are, alas! but dreams.

LXXXVII
The subtle ways of Destiny I know;
In me she plays her game of "Give and Go."
Misfortune I receive in cash, but joy,
In drafts on Heaven or on the winds that blow.

LXXXVIII
I give and go, grim Destiny,—I play
Upon this checker-board of Night and Day
The dark game with thee, but the day will come
When one will turn the Board the other way.

LXXXIX
If my house-swallow, laboring with zest,
Felt like myself the burden of unrest,
Unlightened by inscrutable designs,
She would not build her young that cozy nest.

XC
Thy life with guiltless life-blood do not stain—

Hunt not the children of the woods; in vain
Thou'lt try one day to wash thy bloody hand:
Nor hunter here nor hunted long remain.

XCI

Oh! cast my dust away from thee, and doff
Thy cloak of sycophancy and like stuff:
I'm but a shadow on the sandy waste,—
Enough of thy duplicity, enough!

XCII

Behold! the Veil that hid thy soul is torn
And all thy secrets on the winds are borne:
The hand of Sin has written on thy face
"Awake, for these untimely furrows warn!"

XCIII

A prince of souls, 'tis sung in ancient lay,
One morning sought a vesture of the clay;
He came into the Pottery, the fool—
The lucky fool was warned to stay away.

XCIV

But I was not. Oh! that the Fates decree
That I now cast aside this clay of me;
My soul and body wedded for a while
Are sick and would that separation be.

XCV

"Thou shalt not kill!"—Thy words, O God, we heed,
Though thy two Soul-devouring Angels feed
Thy Promise of another life on this,—
To have spared us both, it were a boon indeed.

XCVI

Oh! that some one would but return to tell
If old Nubakht is burning now in hell,
Or if the workers for the Prophet's prize
Are laughing at his Paradisal sell.

XCVII

Once I have tried to string a few Pearl-seeds
Upon my Rosary of wooden beads;
But I have searched, and I have searched in vain
For pearls in all the caverns of the creeds

XCVIII

And in the palaces of wealth I found

Some beads of wisdom scattered on the ground,
Around the throne of Power, beneath the feet
Of fair-faced slaves with flowers of folly crowned.

XCIX
Thy wealth can shed no tears around thy bier,
Nor can it wash thy hands of shame and fear;
Ere thou departest with it freely part,—
Let others plead for thee and God will hear.

C
For me thy silks and feathers have no charm
The pillow I like best is my right arm;
The comforts of this passing show I spurn,
For Poverty can do the soul no harm.

CI
The guiding hand of Allah I can see
Upon my staff: of what use then is he
Who'd be the blind man's guide? Thou silent oak,
No son of Eve shall walk with me and thee.

CII
My life's the road on which I blindly speed:
My goal's the grave on which I plant a reed
To shape my Hope, but soon the Hand unseen
Will strike, and lo! I'm but a sapless weed.

CIII
O Rabbi, curse us not if we have been
Nursed in the shadow of the Gate of Sin
Built by thy hand—yea, ev'n thine angels blink
When we are coming out and going in.

CIV
And like the dead of Ind I do not fear
To go to thee in flames; the most austere
Angel of fire a softer tooth and tongue
Hath he than dreadful Munker and Nakir.

CV
Now, at this end of Adam's line I stand
Holding my father's life-curse in my hand,
Doing no one the wrong that he did me:—
Ah, would that he were barren as the sand!

CVI
Ay, thus thy children, though they sovereigns be,

When truth upon them dawns, will turn on thee,
Who cast them into life's dark labyrinth
Where even old Izrail can not see.

CVII

And in the labyrinth both son and sire
Awhile will fan and fuel hatred's fire;
Sparks of the log of evil are all men
Allwhere—extinguished be the race entire!

CVIII

If miracles were wrought in ancient years,
Why not to-day, O Heaven-cradled seers?
The highway's strewn with dead, the lepers weep,
If ye but knew,—if ye but saw their tears!

CIX

Fan thou a lisping fire and it will leap
In flames, but dost thou fan an ashy heap?
They would respond, indeed, whom thou dost call,
Were they not dead, alas! or dead asleep.

CX

The way of vice is open as the sky,
The way of virtue's like the needle's eye;
But whether here or there, the eager Soul
Has only two Companions—Whence and Why.

CXI

Whence come, O firmament, thy myriad lights?
Whence comes thy sap, O vineyard of the heights?
Whence comes the perfume of the rose, and whence
The spirit-larva which the body blights?

CXII

Whence does the nettle get its bitter sting?
Whence do the honey bees their honey bring?
Whence our Companions, too—our Whence and Why?
O Soul, I do not know a single thing!

CXIII

How many like us in the ages past
Have blindly soared, though like a pebble cast,
Seeking the veil of mystery to tear,
But fell accurst beneath the burning blast?

CXIV

Why try to con the book of earth and sky,

Why seek the truth which neither you nor I
Can grasp? But Death methinks the secret keeps,
And will impart it to us by and by.

CXV

The Sultan, too, relinquishing his throne
Must wayfare through the darkening dust alone
Where neither crown nor kingdom be, and he,
Part of the Secret, here and there is blown.

CXVI

To clay the mighty Sultan must return
And, chancing, help a praying slave to burn
His midnight oil before the face of Him,
Who of the Sultan makes an incense urn.

CXVII

Turned to a cup, who once the sword of state
Held o'er the head of slave and potentate,
Is now held in the tippler's trembling hand,
Or smashed upon the tavern-floor of Fate.

CXVIII

For this I say, Be watchful of the Cage
Of chance; it opes alike to fool and sage;
Spy on the moment, for to-morrow'll be,
Like yesterday, an obliterated page.

CXIX

Yea, kiss the rosy cheeks of new-born Day,
And hail eternity in every ray
Forming a halo round its infant head,
Illumining thy labyrinthine way.

CXX

But I, the thrice-imprisoned, try to troll
Strains of the song of night, which fill with dole
My blindness, my confinement, and my flesh—
The sordid habitation of my soul.

CXXI

Howbeit, my inner vision heir shall be
To the increasing flames of mystery
Which may illumine yet my prisons all,
And crown the ever living hope of me.

NOTES TO THE QUATRAINS

I

To open a poem with a few amatory lines, is a literary tradition among Arab poets. But Abu'l-Ala, having had no occasion to evince such tender emotions, whether real or merely academic, succeeded, as in everything else he did, in deviating from the trodden path. I find, however, in his minor Diwan, Suct uz-Zand, a slight manifestation of his youthful ardor, of which this and the succeeding quatrains, descriptive of the charms of Night, are fairly representative.

III

"Ahmad," Mohammed the Prophet.

IV

"And hear the others who with cymbals try," etc., meaning the Christians; in the preceding quatrain he referred to the Mohammedans.

VII

Milton, in Il Penseroso, also speaks of night as "the starred Ethiop queen"; and Shakespeare, in Romeo and Juliet, has these lines:

"Her beauty hangs upon the cheek of night
As a rich jewel in an Ethiop ear."
The source of inspiration is the same to all world-poets, who only
differ sometimes in the jars they bring to the source.

XIII

The purple, white, and gray garments, symbolizing Man's dreams of power, of love, and of bliss.

XIV

The same idea is expressed by Omar Khayyam. Here are the first three lines of the 122nd quatrain of Heron-Allen's literal translation:

"To him who understands the mysteries of the world
The joy and sorrow of the world is all the same,
Since the good and the bad of the world all come to an end."

"Howdaj," a sort of palanquin borne by camels; hence, a wedding or a triumphal procession.

XVII

"Thamud" and "'Ad," two of the primitive tribes which figure prominently in the legendary history of Arabia. They flouted and stoned the prophets that were sent to them, and are constantly held up in the Koran as terrible examples of the pride that goeth before destruction.

"Hashem's fearless lad," Mohammed the Prophet.

XVIII

I quote again from Omar, Fitzgerald's translation:

"And this reviving Herb, whose Tender Green

Fledges the River-Lip, on which we lean—
Ah, lean upon it lightly! for who knows
From what once lovely Lip it springs unseen."

In justice to both the Persian and the Arab poet, however, I give the 43d quatrain of Heron-Allen's, which I think contains two lines of that of Fitzgerald, together with Abu'l-Ala's own poetic-fancy.

"Everywhere that there has been a rose or tulip bed
There has been spilled the crimson blood of a king;
Every violet shoot that grows from the earth
Is a mole that was once upon the cheek of beauty."

XX
"Zakkum," a tree which, in Mohammedan mythology, is said to have its roots in hell, and from which are fed the dwellers of hell-fire. In one of the Chapters of the Koran, The Saffat, I find this upon it:

"And is that a pure bounty, or the Zakkum tree? It is a tree which groweth in hell; its fruits are like unto the heads of the devils, who eat from it, and from it fill their stomachs."

Zakkum is also one of the bitter-fruited trees of Arabia. And the people there speak of "a mouthful of zakkum" when they want to describe an unhappy experience. It is also the name of one of the plants of the desert, whose flower is like the jasmine; and of one of the trees of Jericho, whose fruit is like the date, but somewhat bitter.

XXIII
"Jannat," Paradise. "Juhannam," Hell.

XXIX
And Tennyson also says:

"There is more truth in honest doubt,
Believe me, than in all the creeds."

XXXI
"Mutakallem," disputant. The mutakallemin are the logicians and theologians of Islam.

XXXIII
Hadil is a poetic term for dove. And in Arabic mythology it is the name of a particular dove, which died of thirst in the days of Noah, and is bemoaned until this day.

"Ababil," a flock of birds, who scourged with flint-stones which they carried in their beaks, one of the ancient Arab tribes, noted for its idolatry and evil practices.

XXXVIII, XCIII and XCIV
I quote again from Omar, Fitzgerald's version, quatrain 44:

"Why, if the Soul can fling the dust aside,
And naked on the air of Heaven ride,

Were't not a shame—were't not a shame for him
In this clay carcass crippled to abide?"

And from Heron-Allen's, quatrain 145:

"O Soul, if thou canst purify thyself from the dust of the clay,
Thou, naked spirit, canst soar in the heav'ns,
The Empyrian is thy sphere—let it be thy shame
That thou comest and art a dweller within the confines of earth."

XLVIII
"The walking dust was once a thing of stone," is my rendering of the line,

"And he concerning whom the world is puzzled
Is an animal evolved of inorganic matter."

This line of Abu'l-Ala is much quoted by his enthusiastic admirers of the present day to prove that he anticipated Darwin's theory of evolution. And it is remarkable how the fancy of the poet sometimes coincides with the logical conclusions of the scientist.

XLIX
"Iblis," the devil.

L
"Rabbi," my lord God.

LVI
This quatrain is quoted by many of the Biographers of Abu'l-Ala to prove that he is a materialist. Which argument is easily refuted, however, with others quatrains taken at random from the Luzumiyat.

LVII, LVIII and LIX
Omar was also a confessed cynical-hypocrite. Thus runs the first line of the 114th quatrain of Heron-Allen's:

"The world being fleeting I practise naught but artifice."

And he also chafes in the chains of his sins. Following is the 23d quatrain of the same translation:

"Khayyam, why mourn for thy sins?
From grieving thus what advantage more or less dost thou gain?
Mercy was never for him who sins not,
Mercy is granted for sins; why then grieve?"

Abu'l-Ala, in a quatrain which I did not translate, goes even farther in his questioning perplexity. "Why do good since thou art to be forgiven for thy sins?" he asks.

LXII
"Kaaba Stone," the sacred black stone in the Kaaba at Meccah.

LXXVII

The American poet, Lowell, in "The Crisis," utters the same cry:

"Truth forever on the scaffold,
Wrong forever on the throne."

XC

"And the poor beetle that we tread upon
In corporal sufferance finds a pang as great
As when a giant dies."
—Shakespeare: Measure for Measure.

"To let go a flea is a more virtuous act than to give a dirham to a beggar."—Abu'l-Ala.

XCIII and XCIV

Omar too, in the 157th quatrain of Heron-Allen's—

"Had I charge of the matter I would not have come,
And likewise could I control my going, where could I go?"

XCV

"Thy two soul-devouring angels," the angels of death and resurrection.

XCVI

"Nubakht," one of the opponents of the Prophet Mohammed.

CIII

"Rabbi," my lord God.

CIV

"And like the dead of Ind," referring to the practice of the Hindus who burn their dead.

"Munker" and "Nakir," the two angels who on the Day of Judgment open the graves of the dead and cross-examine them—the process is said to be very cruel—as to their faith. Whosoever is found wanting in this is pushed back into the grave and thence thrown into Juhannam. No wonder Abu'l-Ala prefers cremation.

CV

He wrote his own epitaph, which is:

"This wrong to me was by my father done,
But never by me to any one."

CVI

"Izrail," the angel of death.

CXV, CXVI and CXVII

These will suggest to the reader Shakespeare's lines:

"Imperial Caesar, dead and turned to clay,
Might stop a hole to keep the wind away;
O, that that earth, which kept the world in awe,
Should stop a wall t'expel the winter's flaw."

CXVIII
Compare this with Omar's:

"Thou hast no power over the morrow,
And anxiety about the morrow is useless to thee:
Waste not thou the moment, if thy heart is not mad,
For the value of the remainder of thy life is not certain."

NOTES

[1] My learned friend, Count E. de Mulinen, called my attention to the work of Von Kremer on Abu'l-Ala. And I have seen copies of a certain German Asiatic Review in which were published translations, made by that eminent Orientalist, of many poems from the Luzumiyat. He speaks of Abu'l-Ala as one of the greatest moralists of all times, whose profound genius anticipated much that is commonly attributed to the so-called modern spirit of enlightenment.

Professor D. S. Margoliouth has also translated into English the Letters of Abu'l-Ala, which were published with the Arabic Text at the Clarendon Press, Oxford, 1898. Also Professor Raynold A. Nicholson, in his work, "A Literary History of the Arabs," discusses the poet at length and renders into English some poems from the Luzumiyat. A work was published by Charles Carrington, Paris, 1904, under the title, "Un Précurseur d'Omar Khayyam, Le Poéte Aveugle: Extraits de Poémes et de Lettres d'Abu'l-Ala al-Ma'arri." And another, "The Diwan of Abu'l-Ala," done into English by Henry Baerlein, who must have helped himself freely to the Quatrains of Von Kremer.

[2] For a picturesque description of the squalidness and sordidness of Ma'arrah and its people, see Letter XX of "The Letters of Abu'l-Ala," Oxford Edition.

[3] When he visited Baghdad he was about thirty-seven years of age. And when he went to attend a lecture there by one of the leading scholars, he was called by the lecturer, istabl, which is Syrian slang for blind.

[4] "He was four years of age when he had the attack of small-pox. The sight of his left eye was entirely lost and the eyeball of his right had turned white. Al-Hafiz us-Silafi relates: 'Abu Muhammad Abdallah told me that he visited him (Abu'l-Ala) once with his uncle and found him sitting on an old hair matting. He was very old, and the disease that attacked him in his boyhood had left its deep traces on his emaciated face. He bade me come near him and blessed me as he placed his hand on my head. I was a boy then, and I can picture him before me now. I looked into his eyes and remarked how the one was horribly protruding, and the other, buried in its socket, could barely be seen.'"—Ibn Khillikan.

[5] "How long he retained any sort of vision is not certain. His frequent references in his writings to stars, flowers, and the forms of the Arabic letters imply that he could see a little at least some years after this calamity."—D. S. Margoliouth: The Letters of Abu'l-Ala.

"He used to play chess and nard."—Safadi.

[6] For an interesting account of Literary Society in Baghdad see Renan's "Islam and Science"; also the Biography to the Letters of Abu'l-Ala. Prof. Margoliouth, though not unfair in his judgment of the poet, is unnecessarily captious at times. He would seem partial to the suffrage of orthodox Mohammedans with regard to Abu'l-Ala's unorthodox religious views. But they have a reason, these ulama, for endeavoring to keep a genius like Abu'l-Ala within the pale of belief. Which reason, let us hope, has no claim on Prof. Margoliouth. And in his attempt to depreciate Abu'l-Ala as a disinterested and independent scholar and poet, he does not escape the inconsistency which often follows in the wake of cavil. Read this, for instance:

"Like many of those who have failed to secure material prosperity, he found comfort in a system which flatters the vanity of those who have not succeeded by teaching that success is not worth attaining."

And this, not on the same page perhaps, but close to it:

"For though other roads towards obtaining the means of supporting himself at Baghdad have been open to him, that which he refused to follow (the profession of an encomiast, i. e. a sycophant, a toady) was the most certain."

[7] Biography of Abu'l-Ala by Adh-Dhahabi.

[8] "The Letters, which abound in quotations, enable us to gauge the power of his memory better than these wonder-loving narrators."—D. S. Margoliouth.

[9] In one of his poems he speaks of three prisons, his body being the third. Here is Professor Nicholson's translation:

Methink I am thrice-imprisoned—ask not me
Of news that need no telling—
By loss of sight, confinement in my house,
And this vile body for my spirit's dwelling.

[10] Also his Commentary on the works of the poet Al-Mutanabbi.

[11] Adh-Dhahabi gives the titles of forty-eight of his works, to which Safadi adds fourteen. A literary baggage of considerable bulk, had not most of it perished when the Crusaders took Ma'arrah in 1098. Now, the Luzumiyat, the Letters, Suct uz-Zand and the Epistle of Forgiveness can be obtained in printed form.

[12] "What he says of Al-Maghribi in the First Letter became literally true of himself: 'As Sinai derives its fame from Moses and the Stone from Abraham, so Ma'arrah is from this time (after his return from Baghdad) known by him.'"—D. S. Margoliouth.

[13] Even before he visited Baghdad he had a pension of thirty dinars (about $100), half of which he paid to his servant, and the other half was sufficient to secure for him the necessaries of life. "He lived on lentils and figs," says Adh-Dhahabi; "he slept on a felt mattress; he wore nothing but cotton garments; and his dwelling was furnished with a straw matting."

[14] We have the following from Adh-Dhahabi:

"One of these critics came one day to Abu'l-Ala and relating the conversation himself said, 'What is it that is quoted and said about you?' I asked.

'It is false; they are jealous of me,' he replied.

'And what have you to incite their jealousy? You have left for them both this world and the other.'

'And the other?' murmured the poet, questioning, ruminating. 'And the other, too?'"

[15] "His poems, generally known as the Luzumiyat, arrest attention by their boldness and originality as well as by the sombre and earnest tone which pervades them."—Raynold A. Nicholson: A Literary History of the Arabs.

[16] The Governor of Halab, Salih ibn Mirdas, passed once by Ma'arrah, when thirty of its distinguished citizens were imprisoned on account of a riot in the town the previous year. Abu'l-Ala being asked to intercede for them, was led to Salih, who received him most politely and asked him what he desired. The poet, in eloquent but unflattering speech, asked Salih 'to take and give forgiveness.' And the Governor, not displeased, replied: 'I grant it you.' Whereupon the prisoners were released.

[17] "His poems leave no aspect of the age (in which he lived) untouched, and present a vivid picture of degeneracy and corruption, in which tyrannous rulers, venal judges, hypocritical and unscrupulous theologians, swindling astrologers, roving swarms of dervishes and godless Carmathians, occupy a prominent place."—Raynold A. Nicholson: A Literary History of the Arabs.

[18] "The Mohammedan critics who thought he let his opinions be guided by his pen probably came near the truth. And any man who writes in such fetters as the meter (he means the rhyme-ending; for Abu'l-Ala made use of every known meter of Arabic prosody) of the Luzumiyat imposes, can exercise but slight control over his thoughts."—D. S. Margoliouth: Letters of Abu'l-Ala.

[19] This work, of which Professor Nicholson says there are but two copies extant, one in Constantinople and the other in his own Collection, was published in Cairo, in 1907, edited by Sheikh Ibrahim ul-Yazeji.

[20] "To let go a flea is a more virtuous act than to give a dirham to a beggar."—Abu'l-Ala.

[21] The Orthodox, i. e. the Mohammedans.

[22] I do not find these verses in the printed copies of either the Luzumiyat or Suct uz-Zand. But they are quoted, from some Ms. copy I suppose, by the historian Abu'l-Fida.

[23] Omar wrote poetry in Arabic too. My learned friend, Isa Iskandar Maluf of Zehleh, Mt. Lebanon, showed me some quatrains of "Omar the Tent-maker and Astronomer," in an old Arabic Ms. which bear a striking resemblance to some of Abu'l-Ala's both in thought and style.

INTRODUCTION TO THE DIWAN

God help him who has no nails wherewith to scratch himself.
Arabian proverb.

An effort has been made to render in this book some of the poems of Abu'l-Ala the Syrian, who was born 973 years after Jesus Christ and some forty-four before Omar Khayyam. But the life of such a man—his triumph over circumstance, the wisdom he achieved, his unconventionality, his opposition to revealed religion, the sincerity of his religion, his interesting friends at Baghdad and Ma'arri, the multitude of his disciples, his kindliness and cynic pessimism and the reverence which he enjoyed, the glory of his meditations, the renown of his prodigious memory, the fair renown of bending to the toil of public life, not to the laureateship they pressed upon him, but the post of being spokesman at Aleppo for the troubles of his native villagers,—the life of such a one could not be told within the space at our command; it will, with other of his poems, form the subject of a separate volume. What appears advisable is that we should devote this introduction to a commentary on the poems here translated; which we call a "diwan," by the way, because they are selected out of all his works. A commentary on the writings of a modern poet is supposed to be superfluous, but in the days of Abu'l-Ala of Ma'arri you were held to pay the highest compliment if, and you were yourself a poet, you composed a commentary on some other poet's work. Likewise you were held to be a thoughtful person if you gave the world a commentary on your own productions; and Abu'l-Ala did not neglect to write upon his Sikt al-Zand ("The Falling Spark of Tinder") and his Lozum ma la Yalzam ("The Necessity of what is Unnecessary"), out of which our diwan has been chiefly made. But his elucidations have been lost. And we—this nobody will contradict—have lost the old facility. For instance, Hasan ibn Malik ibn Abi Obaidah was one day attending on Mansur the Chamberlain, and he displayed a collection of proverbs which Ibn Sirri had made for the Caliph's delectation. "It is very fine," quoth Mansur, "but it wants a commentary." And Hasan in a week returned with a commentary, very well written, of three hundred couplets. One other observation: we shall not be able to present upon these pages a connected narrative, a dark companion of the poem, which is to the poem as a shadow to the bird. A mediæval Arab would have no desire to see this theory of connection put in practice—no, not even with a poem; for the lines, to win his admiration, would be as a company of stars much more than as a flying bird. Suppose that he produced a poem of a hundred lines, he would perchance make fifty leaps across the universe. But if we frown on such discursiveness, he proudly shows us that the hundred lines are all in rhyme. This Arab and ourselves—we differ so profoundly. "Yet," says he, "if there existed no diversity of sight then would inferior merchandise be left unsold." And when we put his poem into English, we are careless of the hundred rhymes; we paraphrase—"Behold the townsmen," so cried one of the Bedawi, "they have for the desert but a single word, we have a dozen!"—and we reject, as I have done, the quantitative metre, thinking it far preferable if the metre sings itself into an English ear, as much as possible with that effect the poet wants to give; and we oppose ourselves, however unsuccessfully, to his discursiveness by making alterations in the order of the poem. But in this commentary we shall be obliged to leap, like Arabs, from one subject to another. And so let us begin.

With regard to prayer (quatrain 1), the Moslem is indifferent as to whether he perform this function in his chamber or the street, considering that every spot is equally pure for the service of God. And yet the Prophet thought that public worship was to be encouraged; it was not a vague opinion, because he knew it was exactly five-and-twenty times more valuable than private prayer. It is related of al-Muzani that when he missed being present in the mosque he repeated his prayers twenty-five times. "He was a diver for subtle ideas," said the biographer Ibn Khallikan. And although our poet, quoting the Carmathians, here deprecates the common worship, he remarks in one of his letters that he would have gone to mosque on Fridays if he had not fallen victim to an unmentionable complaint. . . . The pre-Islamic Arabs were accustomed to sacrifice sheep (quatrain 1) and other animals in Mecca and elsewhere, at various stones which were regarded as idols or as altars of the gods.[1] Sometimes they killed a human being, such as the four hundred captive nuns of whom we read that they were sacrificed by al-Mundhir to the goddess Aphrodite. Sheep are offered up to-day in Palestine: for instance, if the first wife of a man is barren and the second wife has children, then the former vows that in return for a son she will give a lamb. Apparently when it was thought desirable to be particularly solemn a horse was sacrificed, and this we hear of with the Persians, Indians, and more western people. White was held to be the favourable colour, so we read in Herodotus (i. 189) that the Persians sacrificed white horses. In Sweden it was thought that a black lamb must be dedicated to the water sprite before he would teach any one to play the harp. As for the subsequent fate of the victim, Burton tells us that the Moslems do not look with favour on its being eaten. Unlike them, Siberian Buriats will sacrifice a sheep and boil the mutton and hoist it on a scaffold for the gods, and chant a song and then consume the meat. So, too, the zealous devil-worshippers of Travancore, whose diet is the putrid flesh of cattle and tigers, together with arrak and toddy and rice, which they have previously offered to their deities.

The words of Abu'l-Ala concerning day and night (quatrain 2) may be compared with what he says elsewhere:

These two, young for ever,
Speed into the West—
Our life in their clutches—
And give us no rest.

"Generation goeth and generation cometh," says Ecclesiastes, "while for ever the earth abideth. The sun riseth also and the sun goeth down and cometh panting back to his place where he riseth." . . . The early dawn, the time of scarlet eyes, was also when the caravan would be attacked. However, to this day the rising sun is worshipped by the Bedawi, despite the prohibition of Mahomet and despite the Moslem dictum that the sun rises between the devil's horns. Now the divinity of the stars (quatrain 4) had been affirmed by Plato and Aristotle; it was said that in the heavenly bodies dwelt a ruling intelligence superior to man's, and more lasting.[2] And in Islam, whose holy house, the Kaaba, had traditionally been a temple of Saturn, we notice that the rationalists invariably connect their faith with the worship of Venus and other heavenly bodies. We are told by ash-Shahrastani, in his Book of Religious and Philosophical Sects, that the Indians hold Saturn for the greatest luck, on account of his height and the size of his body. But such was not Abu'l-Ala's opinion. "As numb as Saturn," he writes in one of his letters,[3] "and as dumb as a crab has every one been struck by you." Elsewhere he says in verse:

If dark the night, old Saturn is a flash
Of eyes which threaten from a face of ash.

And the worship of Saturn, with other deities, is about a hundred years later resented by Clotilda, says Gregory of Tours, when she is moving Chlodovich her husband to have their son baptized. When the little boy dies soon after baptism, the husband does not fail to draw a moral. But misfortunes, in the language of an Arab poet, cling about the wretched even as a coat of mail (quatrain 6) is on the warrior. This image was a favourite among the Arabs, and when Ibn Khallikan wants to praise the verses of one As Suli, he informs us that they have the reputation of delivering from sudden evil any person who recites them frequently. When this evil is complete, with rings strongly riven, it passes away while he thinks that nothing can dispel it. . . . We have mention in this quatrain of a winding-sheet, and that could be of linen or of damask. The Caliph Solaiman was so fond of damask that every one, even the cook, was forced to wear it in his presence, and it clothed him in the grave. Yet he, like other Moslems (quatrain 10), would believe that he must undergo the fate recorded in a book. The expression that a man's destiny is written on his forehead, had its origin without a doubt, says Goldziher, in India. We have remarked upon the Indian ideas which had been gathered by Abu'l-Ala at Baghdad. There it was that he enjoyed the opportunity of seeing ships (quatrain 11). He spent a portion of his youth beside the sea, at Tripoli. But in the capital were many boats whose fascination he would not resist,— the Chinese junks laboriously dragged up from Bassora, and dainty gondolas of basket-work covered with asphalt.[4] However, though in this place and in others, very frequently, in fact, Abu'l-Ala makes mention of the sea, his fondness of it was, one thinks, for literary purposes. He writes a letter to explain how grieved he is to hear about a friend who purposes to risk himself upon the sea, and he recalls a certain verse: "Surely it is better to drink among the sand-heaps foul water mixed with pure than to venture on the sea." From Baghdad also he would carry home the Zoroastrian view (quatrain 14) that night was primordial and the light created. As a contrast with these foreign importations, we have reference (quatrain 15) to the lute, which was the finest of Arabian instruments. They said themselves that it was invented by a man who flourished in the year 500 B.C. and added an eighth string to the lyre. Certainly the Arab lute was popular among the Greeks: [Greek: arabion ar' egô kekinêka aulon], says Menander. It was carried to the rest of Europe by crusaders at the beginning of the twelfth century, about which time it first appears in paintings, and its form persisted till about a hundred years ago.[5] But with regard to travels (quatrain 18), in the twenty-seventh letter of Abu'l-Ala, "I observe," says he, "that you find fault with travelling. Why so? Ought not a man to be satisfied with following the precedent set by Moses, who, when he turned towards Midyan, said, Maybe the Lord will guide me?" (Koran 28, 21). Should a man be satisfied with what he hears from the philosopher al-Kindi? "In any single existing thing, if it is thoroughly known, we possess," he said, "a mirror in which we may behold the entire scheme of things" (quatrain 20). The same philosopher has laid it down that, "Verily there is nothing constant in this world of coming and going (quatrain 24), in which we may be deprived at any moment of what we love. Only in the world of reason is stability to be found. If then we desire to see our wishes fulfilled and would not be robbed of what is dear to us, we must turn to the eternal blessings of reason, to the fear of God, to science and to good works. But if we follow merely after material possessions in the belief that we can retain them, we are pursuing an object which does not really exist." . . . And this idea of transitoriness prevails so generally among the Arabs that the salad-seller recommends his transitory wares to pious folk by calling, "God is that which does not pass away!" So, too, the Arab pictures as a bird, a thing of transience, the human soul. In Syria the dove is often carved upon their ancient tombstones. And the Longobards among their graves erected poles in memory of kinsfolk who had died abroad or had been slain in battle; on the summit of the pole was a wooden image of a dove, whose head was pointed in the direction where the loved one lay buried. With us, as with Abu'l-Ala (quatrain 26), the soul may metaphorically be imagined as a bird, but for the European's ancestor it was a thing of sober earnest, as it is to-day to many peoples. Thus the soul of Aristeas was seen to issue from his mouth in the shape of a raven.[6] In Southern Celebes they think that a bridegroom's soul is apt to fly away at marriage, wherefore coloured rice is scattered over him to induce it to remain. And, as a rule, at festivals in South

Celebes rice is strewed on the head of the person in whose honour the festival is held, with the object of detaining his soul, which at such times is in especial danger of being lured away by envious demons.[7] . . . This metaphor was used by Abu'l-Ala in the letter which he wrote on the death of his mother: "I say to my soul, 'This is not your nest, fly away.'" And elsewhere (quatrain 34) Death is represented as a reaper. Says Francis Thompson:

The goodly grain and the sun-flushed sleeper
The reaper reaps, and Time the reaper.

It is interesting to find Death also called a sower, who disseminates weeds among men: "Dô der Tôt sînen Sâmen under si gesœte."

It was an ancient custom of the Arabs when they took an oath of special significance to plunge their hands into a bowl of perfume and distribute it among those who took part in the ceremony. Of the perfumes, musk (quatrain 38) was one which they affected most. Brought commonly from Turkistan, it was, with certain quantities of sandalwood and ambra, made into a perfume. And "the wounds of him who falls in battle and of the martyrs," said Mahomet, "shall on the Day of Judgment be resplendent with vermilion and odorous as musk." This was repeated by Ibnol Faradhi, who in the Kaaba entreated God for martyrdom and, when this prayer was heard, repented having asked. . . . This quatrain goes on to allude to things which can improve by being struck. There is in the third book of a work on cookery (so rare a thing, they tell us, that no MS. of it exists in England or in any other country that can be heard of) an observation by the eighteenth- century editor to the effect that it is a vulgar error to suppose that walnut-trees, like Russian wives, are all the better for a beating; the long poles and stones which are used by boys and others to get the fruit down, for the trees are very high, are used rather out of kindness to themselves than with any regard to the tree that bears it. This valued treatise, we may mention, is ascribed to Cœlius Apicius; its science, learning, and discipline were extremely condemned, and even abhorred by Seneca and the Stoics. . . . Aloes-wood does not emit a perfume until it is burned:

Lo! of hundreds who aspire
Eighties perish—nineties tire!
They who bear up, in spite of wrecks and wracks,
Were season'd by celestial hail of thwacks.

Fortune in this mortal race
Builds on thwackings for its base;
Thus the All-Wise doth make a flail a staff,
And separates his heavenly corn from chaff.[8]

Reward may follow on such absolute obedience (quatrain 40). We remember what is said by Fra Giovanni in the prison of Viterbo[9]: "Endurez, souffrez, acceptez, veuillez ce que Dieu veut, et votre volonté sera faite sur la terre comme au ciel." And perhaps the dawn for you may be your camel's dawn (quatrain 41); it was usual for Arabs on the point of death to say to their sons: "Bury my steed with me, so that when I rise from the grave I will not have to go on foot." The camel was tied with its head towards its hind legs, a saddle-cloth was wrapped about its neck, and it was left beside the grave until it died. Meanwhile, if the master is a true believer, says Mahomet, his soul has been divided from the body by Azrael, the angel of death. Afterwards the body is commanded to sit upright in the grave, there to be examined by the two black angels, Monkar and Nakyr (quatrain 42), with regard to his faith, the unity of God and the mission of Mahomet. If the answers be correct, the body stays in peace and is refreshed by the air of paradise; if incorrect, these angels beat the corpse upon his temples with iron maces, until he roars out for anguish so loudly that he is heard by all from east to west, except by men and jinn. Abu'l-Ala had little confidence in these two angels; he reminds one of St. Catherine of Sienna, a visionary with uncommon sense, who at the age of eight ran off one afternoon to be a hermit. She was careful to provide herself with bread and water, fearing that the angels would forget to bring her food, and at nightfall she ran home again because she was afraid her parents would be anxious. With regard to the angel of death, Avicenna has related that the soul, like a bird, escapes with much trouble from the snares of earth (quatrain 43), until this angel delivers it from the last of its fetters. We think of the goddess Rân with her net. Death is imagined (quatrain 44) as a fowler or fisher of men, thus: "Dô kam der Tôt als ein diep, und stal dem reinen wîbe daz leben ûz ir lîbe."[10]

On account of its brilliance a weapon's edge (quatrain 46) has been compared in Arab poetry with sunlit glass, with the torch of a monk, with the stars and with the flame in a dark night. Nor would an Arab turn to picturesque comparisons in poetry alone. Speaking of a certain letter, Abu'l-Ala assures the man who wrote it that "it proceeds from the residence of the great doctor who holds the reins of prose and verse" (quatrain 50). Now with regard to glass, it was a very ancient industry among the Arabs. In the second century of the Hegira it was so far advanced that they could make enamelled glass and unite in one glass different colours. A certain skilled chemist of the period was not only expert in these processes (quatrain 52), but even tried to make of glass false pearls, whereon he published a pamphlet.

Death, from being a silent messenger who punctually fulfilled his duty, became a grasping, greedy foe (quatrain 56). In the Psalms (xci. 3-6) he comes as a hunter with snares and arrows. Also "der Tôt wil mit mir ringen."[11] In ancient times Death was not a being that slew, but simply one that fetched away to the underworld, a messenger. So was the soul of the beggar fetched away by angels and carried into Abraham's bosom. An older view was the death-goddess, who receives the dead men in her house and does not fetch them. They are left alone to begin the long and gloomy journey, provided with various things.[12] "Chacun remonte à son tour le calvaire des siècles. Chacun retrouve les peines, chacun retrouve l'espoir désespéré et la folie des siècles. Chacun remet ses pas dans les pas de ceux qui furent, de ceux qui luttèrent avant lui contre la mort, nièrant la mort,—sont morts"[13] (quatrain 57). It is the same for men and trees (quatrain 59). This vision of Abu'l-Ala's is to be compared with Milton's "men as trees walking," a kind of second sight, a blind man's pageant. In reference to haughty folk, an Arab proverb says that "There is not a poplar which has reached its Lord." But on the other hand, "There are some virtues which dig their own graves,"[14] and with regard to excessive polishing of swords (quatrain 60) we have the story of the poet Abu Tammam, related by Ibn Khallikan. He tells us how the poet once recited verses in the presence of some people, and how one of them was a philosopher who said, "This man will not live long, for I have seen in him a sharpness of wit and penetration and intelligence. From this I know that the mind will consume the body, even as a sword of Indian steel eats through its scabbard." Still, in Arabia, where swords were so generally used that a priest would strap one to his belt before he went into the pulpit, there was no unanimous opinion as to the polishing,—which, by the way, was done with wood. A poet boasted that his sword was often or was rarely polished, according as he wished to emphasise the large amount of work accomplished or the excellence of the polishing. Imru'al-Kais says that his sword does not recall the day when it was polished. Another poet says his sword is polished every day and "with a fresh tooth bites off the people's heads."[15] This vigour of expression was not only used for concrete subjects. There exists a poem, dating from a little time before Mahomet, which says that cares (quatrain 62) are like the camels, roaming in the daytime on the distant pastures and at night returning to the camp. They would collect as warriors round the flag. It was the custom for each family to have a flag (quatrain 65), a cloth fastened to a lance, round which it gathered. Mahomet's big standard was called the Eagle,—and, by the bye, his seven swords had names, such as "possessor of the spine."

With quatrain 68 we may compare the verses of a Christian poet, quoted by Tabari:

And where is now the lord of Hadr, he that built it and laid taxes on the land of Tigris?
A house of marble he established, whereof the covering was
made of plaster; in the galbes were nests of birds.
He feared no sorry fate. See, the dominion of him has departed.
Loneliness is on his threshold.

"Consider how you treat the poor," said Dshafer ben Mahomet, who pilgrimaged from Mecca to Baghdad between fifty and sixty times; "they are the treasures of this world, the keys of the other." Take care lest it befall you as the prince (quatrain 69) within whose palace now the wind is reigning. "If a prince would be successful," says Machiavelli, "it is requisite that he should have a spirit capable of turns and variations, in accordance with the variations of the wind." Says an Arab mystic, "The sighing of a poor man for that which he can never reach has more of value than the praying of a rich man through a thousand years." And in connection with this quatrain we may quote Blunt's rendering of Zohair:

I have learned that he who giveth nothing, deaf to his
friends' begging,
loosed shall be to the world's tooth-strokes: fools'
feet shall tread on him.

As for the power of the weak, we have some instances from Abbaside history. One of the caliphs wanted to do deeds of violence in Baghdad. Scornfully he asked of his opponents if they could prevent him. "Yes," they answered, "we will fight you with the arrows of the night." And he desisted from his plans. Prayers, complaints, and execrations which the guiltless, fighting his oppressor, sends up to heaven are called the arrows of the night and are, the Arabs tell us, invariably successful. This belief may solace you for the foundation of suffering (quatrain 71), which, by the way, is also in the philosophic system of Zeno the Stoic. Taking the four elements of Empedocles, he says that three of them are passive, or suffering, elements while only fire is active, and that not wholly. It was Zeno's opinion that everything must be active or must suffer. . . . An explanation for our suffering is given by Soame Jenyns, who flourished in the days when, as his editor could write, referring to his father Sir Roger Jenyns, "the order of knighthood was received by gentlemen with the profoundest gratitude." Soame's thesis is his "Free Inquiry into the Nature and Origin of Evil," that human sufferings are compensated by the enjoyment possibly experienced by some higher order of beings which inflict them, is ridiculed by Samuel Johnson. We have Jenyns's assurance that

To all inferior animals 'tis given
To enjoy the state allotted them by Heav'n.

And (quatrain 75) we may profitably turn to Coleridge:

Oh, what a wonder seems the fear of death!
Seeing how gladly we all sink to sleep;
Babes, children, youths and men,
Night following night, for threescore years and ten.

We should be reconciled, says Abu'l-Ala (quatrain 76), even to the Christian kings of Ghassan, in the Hauran. These were the hereditary enemies of the kings of Hirah. On behalf of the Greek emperors of Constantinople they controlled the Syrian Arabs. But they disappeared before the triumphant Moslems, the last of their kings being Jabalah II., who was dethroned in the year 637. His capital was Bosra, on the road between the Persian Gulf and the Mediterranean. Nowadays the district is chiefly occupied by nomads; to the Hebrews it was known as Bashan, famous for its flocks and oak plantations. We can still discern the traces of troglodyte dwellings of this epoch. The afore-mentioned Jabalah was a convert to Islam, but, being insulted by a Mahometan, he returned to Christianity and betook himself to Constantinople, where he died. But in the time of Abu'l-Ala, the Ghassanites were again in the exercise of authority. "These were the kings of Ghassan," says Abu'l-Ala, "who followed the course of the dead; each of them is now but a tale that is told, and God knows who is good." A poet is a liar, say the Arabs, and the greatest poet is the greatest liar. But in this case Abu'l-Ala in prose was not so truthful as in poetry; for if Jabalah's house had vanished, the Ghassanites were still a power. The poet, for our consolation, has a simile (quatrain 77) that may be put against a passage of Homer:

As with autumnal harvests cover'd o'er,
And thick bestrown, lies Ceres' sacred floor,
When round and round, with never-weary'd pain
The trampling steers beat out th' unnumber'd grain:
So the fierce coursers, as the chariot rolls,
Tread down whole ranks, and crush out heroes' souls.[16]

For everything there is decay, and (quatrain 78) for the striped garment of a long cut which now we are unable to identify.

We read in the Wisdom of Solomon: "As when an arrow is shot at a mark, it parteth the air which immediately cometh together again, so that a man cannot know where it went through." In this place (quatrain 84), if the weapon's road of air is not in vain it will discover justice in the sky. How much the Arabs were averse from frigid justice is to be observed in the matter of recompense for slaying. There existed a regular tariff—so many camels or dates—but they looked askance upon the person who was willing to accept this and forgo his vengeance. If a man was anxious to accept a gift as satisfaction and at the same time to escape reproach, he shot an arrow into the air. Should it come down unspotted, he was able to accept the gift; if it was bloody, then he was obliged to seek for blood. The Arabs, by the way, had been addicted to an ancient game, but Islam tried to stamp this out, like other joys of life. The players had ten arrows, which they shot into the air; seven of them bestowed a right to the portion of a camel, the other three did not. Abu'l-Ala was fond of using arrows metaphorically. "And if one child," he writes to a distinguished sheikh, "were to ask another in the dead of night in a discussion: 'Who is rewarded for staying at home many times what he would be rewarded for going on either pilgrimage?' and the second lad answered: 'Mahomet, son of Sa'id,' his arrow would have fallen near the mark; for your protection of your subjects (quatrain 86) is a greater duty than either pilgrimage." And our poet calls to mind some benefits attached to slavery (quatrain 88): for an offence against morals a slave could receive fifty blows, whereas the punishment of a freeman was double. A married person who did not discharge his vows was liable to be stoned to death, whereas a slave in similar circumstances was merely struck a certain number of blows. It was and still is customary, says von Kremer, if anything is broken by a slave, forthwith to curse Satan, who is supposed to concern himself in very trifling matters. The sympathy Abu'l-Ala displays for men of small possessions may be put beside the modicum (quatrain 92) he wanted for himself. And these necessaries of Abu'l-Ala, the ascetic, must appeal to us as more sincerely felt than those of Ibn at-Ta'awizi, who was of opinion that when seven things are collected together in the drinking-room it is not reasonable to stay away. The list is as follows: a melon, honey, roast meat, a young girl, wax lights, a singer, and wine. But Ibn at-Ta'awizi was a literary person, and in Arabic the names of all these objects begin with the same letter. Abu'l-Ala was more inclined to celebrate the wilderness. He has portrayed (quatrain 93) a journey in the desert where a caravan, in order to secure itself against surprises, is accustomed to send on a spy, who scours the country from the summit of a hill or rock. Should he perceive a sign of danger, he will wave his hand in warning. From Lebid's picture of another journey—which the pre-Islamic poet undertook to the coast lands of Hajar on the Persian Gulf—we learn that when they entered a village he and his party were greeted by the crowing of cocks and the shaking of wooden rattles (quatrain 95), which in the Eastern Christian Churches are substituted for bells. . . . And the mediæval leper, in his grey gown, was obliged to hold a similar object, waving it about and crying as he went: "Unclean! unclean!"

An ambitious man desired, regardless of expense, to hand down his name to posterity (quatrain 99). "Write your name in a prayer," said Epictetus, "and it will remain after you." "But I would have a crown of gold," was the reply. "If you have quite made up your mind to have a crown," said Epictetus, "take a crown of roses, for it is more beautiful." In the words of Heredia:

Déjà le Temps brandit l'arme fatale. As-tu
L'espoir d'éterniser le bruit de ta vertu?
Un vil lierre suffit à disjoindre un trophée;

Et seul, aux blocs épars des marbres triomphaux
Où ta gloire en ruine est par l'herbe étouffée,
Quelque faucheur Samnite ébréchera sa faulx.

Would we write our names so that they endure for ever? There was in certain Arab circles a heresy which held that the letters of the alphabet (quatrain 101) are metamorphoses of men. And Magaira, who founded a sect, maintained that the letters of the alphabet are like limbs of God. According to him, when God wished to create the world, He wrote with His own hands the deeds of men, both the good and the bad; but, at sight of the sins which men were going to commit, He entered into such a fury that He sweated, and from His sweat two seas were formed, the one of salt water and the other of sweet water. From the first one the infidels were formed, and from the second the Shi'ites. But to this view of the everlasting question you may possibly prefer what is advanced (quatrains 103-7) and paraphrased as an episode: Whatever be the wisdom of the worms, we bow before the silence of the rose. As for Abu'l-Ala, we leave him now prostrated (quatrain 108) before the silence of the rolling world. It is a splendour that was seen by Alfred de Vigny:

Je roule avec dédain, sans voir et sans entendre,
A côté des fourmis les populations;
Je ne distingue pas leur terrier de leur cendre.
J'ignore en les portant les noms des nations.
On me dit une mère et je suis une tombe.
Mon hiver prend vos morts comme son hécatombe,
Mon printemps n'entend pas vos adorations.

Avant vous j'étais belle et toujours parfumée,
J'abandonnais au vent mes cheveux tout entiers. . . .

Footnotes

[1] Cf. Lyall, Ancient Arabian Poets.

[2] Cf. Whittaker, The Neo-Platonists.

[3] Of course I use Professor Margoliouth's superb edition of the letters.

[4] Cf. Thielmann, Streifzüge im Kaukasus, etc.

[5] Cf. Ambros, Geschichte der Musik, 1862.

[6] Cf. Pliny, Nat. Hist., vii. 174.

[7] Frazer, The Golden Bough, vol. i., p. 254.

[8] Meredith, The Shaving of Shagpat.

[9] Anatole France, Le Puits de Sainte Claire.

[10] Quoted by Grimm, Teutonic Mythology, vol. 2, p. 845.

[11] Stoufenb., 1126.

[12] Cf. in Scandinavia the death-goddess Hel.

[13] Romain Rolland, Jean Christophe.

[14] Ella d'Arcy, Modern Instances.

[15] Dr. Friedrich Wilhelm Schwarzlose, Die Waffen der alten Araber, aus ihren Dichtern dargestellt.

[16] Pope, Iliad, xx. 577.

THE DIWAN OF ABU'L-ALA

I

Abandon worship in the mosque and shrink
From idle prayer, from sacrificial sheep,
For Destiny will bring the bowl of sleep
Or bowl of tribulation—you shall drink.

II

The scarlet eyes of Morning are pursued
By Night, who growls along the narrow lane;
But as they crash upon our world the twain
Devour us and are strengthened for the feud.

III

Vain are your dreams of marvellous emprise,
Vainly you sail among uncharted spaces,
Vainly seek harbour in this world of faces
If it has been determined otherwise.

IV

Behold, my friends, there is reserved for me
The splendour of our traffic with the sky:
You pay your court to Saturn, whereas I
Am slain by One far mightier than he.

V

You that must travel with a weary load
Along this darkling, labyrinthine street—
Have men with torches at your head and feet
If you would pass the dangers of the road.

VI

So shall you find all armour incomplete
And open to the whips of circumstance,
That so shall you be girdled of mischance
Till you be folded in the winding-sheet.

VII

Have conversation with the wind that goes
Bearing a pack of loveliness and pain:
The golden exultation of the grain
And the last, sacred whisper of the rose

VIII

But if in some enchanted garden bloom
The rose imperial that will not fade,
Ah! shall I go with desecrating spade
And underneath her glories build a tomb?

IX

Shall I that am as dust upon the plain
Think with unloosened hurricanes to fight?
Or shall I that was ravished from the night
Fall on the bosom of the night again?

X

Endure! and if you rashly would unfold
That manuscript whereon our lives are traced,
Recall the stream which carols thro' the waste
And in the dark is rich with alien gold.

XI

Myself did linger by the ragged beach,
Whereat wave after wave did rise and curl;
And as they fell, they fell—I saw them hurl
A message far more eloquent than speech:

XII

We that with song our pilgrimage beguile,
With purple islands which a sunset bore,
We, sunk upon the sacrilegious shore,
May parley with oblivion awhile.

XIII

I would not have you keep nor idly flaunt
What may be gathered from the gracious land,
But I would have you sow with sleepless hand
The virtues that will balance your account.

XIV

The days are dressing all of us in white,
For him who will suspend us in a row.
But for the sun there is no death. I know
The centuries are morsels of the night.

XV

A deed magnanimous, a noble thought
Are as the music singing thro' the years
When surly Time the tyrant domineers
Against the lute where out of it was wrought.

XVI

Now to the Master of the World resign
Whatever touches you, what is prepared,
For many sons of wisdom are ensnared
And many fools in happiness recline.

 XVII

Long have I tarried where the waters roll
From undeciphered caverns of the main,
And I have searched, and I have searched in vain,
Where I could drown the sorrows of my soul.

XVIII

If I have harboured love within my breast,
'Twas for my comrades of the dusty day,
Who with me watched the loitering stars at play,
Who bore the burden of the same unrest.

XIX

For once the witcheries a maiden flung—
Then afterwards I knew she was the bride
Of Death; and as he came, so tender-eyed,
I—I rebuked him roundly, being young.

XX

Yet if all things that vanish in their noon
Are but the part of some eternal scheme,
Of what the nightingale may chance to dream
Or what the lotus murmurs to the moon!

XXI

Have I not heard sagacious ones repeat
An irresistibly grim argument:
That we for all our blustering content
Are as the silent shadows at our feet.

XXII

Aye, when the torch is low and we prepare
Beyond the notes of revelry to pass—
Old Silence will keep watch upon the grass,
The solemn shadows will assemble there.

XXIII

No Sultan at his pleasure shall erect
A dwelling less obedient to decay
Than I, whom all the mysteries obey,
Build with the twilight for an architect.

XXIV

Dark leans to dark! the passions of a man
Are twined about all transitory things,
For verily the child of wisdom clings
More unto dreamland than Arabistan.

XXV

Death leans to death! nor shall your vigilance
Prevent him from whate'er he would possess,
Nor, brother, shall unfilial peevishness
Prevent you from the grand inheritance.

XXVI

Farewell, my soul!—bird in the narrow jail
Who cannot sing. The door is opened! Fly!
Ah, soon you stop, and looking down you cry
The saddest song of all, poor nightingale.

XXVII

Our fortune is like mariners to float
Amid the perils of dim waterways;
Shall then our seamanship have aught of praise
If the great anchor drags behind the boat?

XXVIII

Ah! let the burial of yesterday,
Of yesterday be ruthlessly decreed,
And, if you will, refuse the mourner's reed,
And, if you will, plant cypress in the way.

XXIX

As little shall it serve you in the fight
If you remonstrate with the storming seas,
As if you querulously sigh to these
Of some imagined haven of delight.

XXX

Steed of my soul! when you and I were young
We lived to cleave as arrows thro' the night,—
Now there is ta'en from me the last of light,
And wheresoe'er I gaze a veil is hung.

XXXI

No longer as a wreck shall I be hurled
Where beacons lure the fascinated helm,
For I have been admitted to the realm
Of darkness that encompasses the world.

XXXII

Man has been thought superior to the swarm
Of ruminating cows, of witless foals
Who, crouching when the voice of thunder rolls,
Are banqueted upon a thunderstorm.

XXXIII

But shall the fearing eyes of humankind
Have peeped beyond the curtain and excel
The boldness of a wondering gazelle
Or of a bird imprisoned in the wind?

XXXIV

Ah! never may we hope to win release
Before we that unripeness overthrow,—
So must the corn in agitation grow
Before the sickle sings the songs of peace.

XXXV

Lo! there are many ways and many traps
And many guides, and which of them is lord?
For verily Mahomet has the sword,
And he may have the truth—perhaps! perhaps!

XXXVI

Now this religion happens to prevail
Until by that religion overthrown,—
Because men dare not live with men alone,
But always with another fairy-tale.

XXXVII

Religion is a charming girl, I say;
But over this poor threshold will not pass,
For I may not unveil her, and alas!
The bridal gift I can't afford to pay.

XXXVIII

I have imagined that our welfare is
Required to rise triumphant from defeat;
And so the musk, which as the more you beat,
Gives ever more delightful fragrancies.

XXXIX

For as a gate of sorrow-land unbars
The region of unfaltering delight,
So may you gather from the fields of night
That harvest of diviner thought, the stars.

XL

Send into banishment whatever blows
Across the waves of your tempestuous heart;
Let every wish save Allah's wish depart,
And you will have ineffable repose.

XLI

My faith it is that all the wanton pack
Of living shall be—hush, poor heart!—withdrawn,
As even to the camel comes a dawn
Without a burden for his wounded back.

XLII

If there should be some truth in what they teach
Of unrelenting Monkar and Nakyr,
Before whose throne all buried men appear—
Then give me to the vultures, I beseech.

XLIII

Some yellow sand all hunger shall assuage
And for my thirst no cloud have need to roll,
And ah! the drooping bird which is my soul
No longer shall be prisoned in the cage.

XLIV

Life is a flame that flickers in the wind,
A bird that crouches in the fowler's net—
Nor may between her flutterings forget
That hour the dreams of youth were unconfined.

XLV

There was a time when I was fain to guess
The riddles of our life, when I would soar
Against the cruel secrets of the door,
So that I fell to deeper loneliness.

XLVI

One is behind the draperies of life,
One who will tear these tanglements away—
No dark assassin, for the dawn of day
Leaps out, as leapeth laughter, from the knife.

XLVII

If you will do some deed before you die,
Remember not this caravan of death,
But have belief that every little breath
Will stay with you for an eternity.

XLVIII

Astrologers!—give ear to what they say!
"The stars be words; they float on heaven's breath
And faithfully reveal the days of death,
And surely will reveal that longer day."

XLIX

I shook the trees of knowledge. Ah! the fruit
Was fair upon the bleakness of the soil.
I filled a hundred vessels with my spoil,
And then I rested from the grand pursuit.

L

Alas! I took me servants: I was proud
Of prose and of the neat, the cunning rhyme,
But all their inclination was the crime
Of scattering my treasure to the crowd.

LI

And yet—and yet this very seed I throw
May rise aloft, a brother of the bird,
Uncaring if his melodies are heard—
Or shall I not hear anything below?

LII

The glazier out of sounding Erzerûm,
Frequented us and softly would conspire
Upon our broken glass with blue-red fire,
As one might lift a pale thing from the tomb.

LIII

He was the glazier out of Erzerûm,
Whose wizardry would make the children cry—
There will be no such wizardry when I
Am broken by the chariot-wheels of Doom.

LIV

The chariot-wheels of Doom! Now, hear them roll
Across the desert and the noisy mart,
Across the silent places of your heart—
Smile on the driver you will not cajole.

LV

I never look upon the placid plain
But I must think of those who lived before
And gave their quantities of sweat and gore,
And went and will not travel back again.

LVI

Aye! verily, the fields of blandishment
Where shepherds meditate among their cattle,
Those are the direst of the fields of battle,
For in the victor's train there is no tent.

LVII

Where are the doctors who were nobly fired
And loved their toil because we ventured not,
Who spent their lives in searching for the spot
To which the generations have retired?

LVIII

"Great is your soul,"—these are the words they preach,—
"It passes from your framework to the frame
Of others, and upon this road of shame
Turns purer and more pure."—Oh, let them teach!

LIX

I look on men as I would look on trees,
That may be writing in the purple dome
Romantic lines of black, and are at home
Where lie the little garden hostelries.

LX

Live well! Be wary of this life, I say;
Do not o'erload yourself with righteousness.
Behold! the sword we polish in excess,
We gradually polish it away.

LXI

God who created metal is the same
Who will devour it. As the warriors ride
With iron horses and with iron pride—
Come, let us laugh into the merry flame.

LXII

But for the grandest flame our God prepares
The breast of man, which is the grandest urn;
Yet is that flame so powerless to burn
Those butterflies, the swarm of little cares.

LXIII

And if you find a solitary sage
Who teaches what is truth—ah, then you find
The lord of men, the guardian of the wind,
The victor of all armies and of age.

LXIV

See that procession passing down the street,
The black and white procession of the days—
Far better dance along and bawl your praise
Than if you follow with unwilling feet.

LXV

But in the noisy ranks you will forget
What is the flag. Oh, comrade, fall aside
And think a little moment of the pride
Of yonder sun, think of the twilight's net.

LXVI

The songs we fashion from our new delight
Are echoes. When the first of men sang out,
He shuddered, hearing not alone the shout
Of hills but of the peoples in the night.

LXVII

And all the marvels that our eyes behold
Are pictures. There has happened some event
For each of them, and this they represent—
Our lives are like a tale that has been told.

LXVIII

There is a palace, and the ruined wall
Divides the sand, a very home of tears,
And where love whispered of a thousand years
The silken-footed caterpillars crawl.

LXIX

And where the Prince commanded, now the shriek
Of wind is flying through the court of state:
"Here," it proclaims, "there dwelt a potentate
Who could not hear the sobbing of the weak."

LXX

Beneath our palaces the corner-stone
Is quaking. What of noble we possess,
In love or courage or in tenderness,
Can rise from our infirmities alone.

LXXI

We suffer—that we know, and that is all
Our knowledge. If we recklessly should strain
To sweep aside the solid rocks of pain,
Then would the domes of love and courage fall.

LXXII

But there is one who trembles at the touch
Of sorrow less than all of you, for he
Has got the care of no big treasury,
And with regard to wits not overmuch.

LXXIII

I think our world is not a place of rest,
But where a man may take his little ease,
Until the landlord whom he never sees
Gives that apartment to another guest.

LXXIV

Say that you come to life as 'twere a feast,
Prepared to pay whatever is the bill
Of death or tears or—surely, friend, you will
Not shrink at death, which is among the least?

LXXV

Rise up against your troubles, cast away
What is too great for mortal man to bear.
But seize no foolish arms against the share
Which you the piteous mortal have to pay.

LXXVI

Be gracious to the King. You cannot feign
That nobody was tyrant, that the sword
Of justice always gave the just award
Before these Ghassanites began to reign.

LXXVII

You cultivate the ranks of golden grain,
He cultivates the cavaliers. They go
With him careering on some other foe,
And your battalions will be staunch again.

LXXVIII

The good law and the bad law disappear
Below the flood of custom, or they float
And, like the wonderful Sar'aby coat,
They captivate us for a little year.

LXXIX

God pities him who pities. Ah, pursue
No longer now the children of the wood;
Or have you not, poor huntsman, understood
That somebody is overtaking you?

LXXX

God is above. We never shall attain
Our liberty from hands that overshroud;
Or can we shake aside this heavy cloud
More than a slave can shake aside the chain?

LXXXI

"There is no God save Allah!"—that is true,
Nor is there any prophet save the mind
Of man who wanders through the dark to find
The Paradise that is in me and you.

LXXXII

The rolling, ever-rolling years of time
Are as a diwan of Arabian song;
The poet, headstrong and supremely strong,
Refuses to repeat a single rhyme.

LXXXIII

An archer took an arrow in his hand;
So fair he sent it singing to the sky
That he brought justice down from—ah, so high!
He was an archer in the morning land.

LXXXIV

The man who shot his arrow from the west
Made empty roads of air; yet have I thought
Our life was happier until we brought
This cold one of the skies to rule the nest.

LXXXV

Run! follow, follow happiness, the maid
Whose laughter is the laughing waterfall;
Run! call to her—but if no maiden call,
'Tis something to have loved the flying shade.

LXXXVI

You strut in piety the while you take
That pilgrimage to Mecca. Now beware,
For starving relatives befoul the air,
And curse, O fool, the threshold you forsake.

LXXXVII

How man is made! He staggers at the voice,
The little voice that leads you to the land
Of virtue; but, on hearing the command
To lead a giant army, will rejoice.

LXXXVIII

Behold the cup whereon your slave has trod;
That is what every cup is falling to.
Your slave—remember that he lives by you,
While in the form of him we bow to God.

LXXXIX

The lowliest of the people is the lord
Who knows not where each day to make his bed,
Whose crown is kept upon the royal head
By that poor naked minister, the sword.

XC

Which is the tyrant? say you. Well, 'tis he
That has the vine-leaf strewn among his hair
And will deliver countries to the care
Of courtesans—but I am vague, you see.

XCI

The dwellers of the city will oppress
Your days: the lion, a fight-thirsty fool,
The fox who wears the robe of men that rule—
So run with me towards the wilderness.

XCII

Our wilderness will be the laughing land,
Where nuts are hung for us, where nodding peas
Are wild enough to press about our knees,
And water fills the hollow of our hand.

XCIII

My village is the loneliness, and I
Am as the travellers through the Syrian sand,
That for a moment see the warning hand
Of one who breasted up the rock, their spy.

XCIV

Where is the valiance of the folk who sing
These valiant stories of the world to come?
Which they describe, forsooth! as if it swum
In air and anchored with a yard of string.

XCV

Two merchantmen decided they would battle,
To prove at last who sold the finest wares;
And while Mahomet shrieked his call to prayers,
The true Messiah waved his wooden rattle.

XCVI

Perchance the world is nothing, is a dream,
And every noise the dreamland people say
We sedulously note, and we and they
May be the shadows flung by what we seem.

XCVII

Zohair the poet sang of loveliness
Which is the flight of things. Oh, meditate
Upon the sorrows of our earthly state,
For what is lovely we may not possess.

XCVIII

Heigho! the splendid air is full of wings,
And they will take us to the—friend, be wise
For if you navigate among the skies
You too may reach the subterranean kings.

XCIX

Now fear the rose! You travel to the gloom
Of which the roses sing and sing so fair,
And, but for them, you'd have a certain share
In life: your name be read upon the tomb.

C

There is a tower of silence, and the bell
Moves up—another man is made to be.
For certain years they move in company,
But you, when fails your song do fail as well.

CI

No sword will summon Death, and he will stay
For neither helm nor shield his falling rod.
We are the crooked alphabet of God,
And He will read us ere he wipes away.

CII

How strange that we, perambulating dust,
Should be the vessels of eternal fire,
That such unfading passion of desire
Should be within our fading bodies thrust.

CIII

Deep in a silent chamber of the rose
There was a fattened worm. He looked around,
Espied a relative and spoke at him:
It seems to me this world is very good.

CIV

A most unlovely world, said brother worm,
For all of us are piteous prisoners.
And if, declared the first, your thought is true,
And this a prison be, melikes it well.

CV

So well that I shall weave a song of praise
And thankfulness because the world was wrought
For us and with such providential care—
My brother, I will shame you into singing.

CVI

Then, cried the second, I shall raise a voice
And see what poor apologies are made.
And so they sang, these two, for many days,
And while they sang the rose was beautiful.

CVII

But this affected not the songful ones,
And evermore in beauty lived the rose.
And when the worms were old and wiser too,
They fell to silence and humility.

CVIII

A night of silence! 'Twas the swinging sea
And this our world of darkness. And the twain
Rolled on below the stars; they flung a chain
Around the silences which are in me.

CIX

The shadows come, and they will come to bless
Their brother and his dwelling and his fame,
When I shall soil no more with any blame
Or any praise the silence I possess.

APPENDIX

ON THE NAME ABU'L-ALA

Arab names have always been a stumbling-block, and centuries ago there was a treatise written which was called "The Tearing of the Veil from before Names and Patronymics." Abu Bakr Ahmad ibn Jarit al-Misri is a fair example of the nomenclature; here we have the patronymic (Abu Bakr—father of Bakr), the personal name (Ahmad), the surname (ibn Jarit—son of Jarit), and the ethnic name (al-Misri—native of Egypt). In addition, they made use of fancy names if they were poets (such as Ssorrdorr, the sack of pearls, who died in the year 1072), names connoting kindred, habitation (such as Ahmad al-Maidani, the great collector of proverbs, who lived near the Maidan, the race-course of Naisapur), faith or trade or personal defects (such as a caliph who was called the father of flies, since on account of his offensive breath no fly would rest upon his lip), and finally they gave each other names of honour (such as sword of the empire, helper of the empire, etc.). Then the caliph gave, as a distinction, double titles and, when these became too common, triple titles. ("In this way," says al-Biruni, "the matter is opposed to sense and clumsy to the last degree, so that a man who says the titles is fatigued when he has scarcely started and he runs the risk of being late for prayer.") . . . The patronymic was, of all of these, the most in favour. At first it was assumed when the eldest son was born; when Bakr came into the world his father took the name of Abu Bakr, and acquired a new importance. This was not by any means peculiar to the Arabs: "O Queen," says Das, a king of Indian folk-song, "O Queen, the name of childless has departed from me." When the Arab had no son, he used an honorific patronymic (such as Abu'l-Ala, father of excellence, or Abu'l-Feda, father of redemption). At times this manufactured patronymic was a thing of mockery, more or less gentle (such as a companion of the Prophet who was fond of cats, and was entitled "father of the cat"). The prevalence among the Arabs of the patronymic is immediately noticed, (a camel is the father of Job; a strongly built person is the father of the locust; a licentious person is the father of the night; and there are multitudes of such formations). . . . With regard to surnames, it was not the custom always for them to denote that so-and-so was the son of his father's family. "Who is your father?" says an Arab to the mule, and he replies, "The horse is my maternal uncle." So there are some people who, for shame, prefer that we should think of them as members of their mother's family. . . .

The following additional quatrains may be quoted:

Unasking have we come,—too late, too soon
Unasking from this plot of earth are sent.
But we, the sons of noble discontent,
Use half our lives in asking for the moon.

("We all sorely complain," says Seneca, "of the shortness of time, and yet have much more than we know what to do with. Our lives are either spent in doing nothing at all or in doing nothing to the purpose, or in doing nothing that we ought to do. We are always complaining that our days are few, and acting as though there would be no end of them.")

So then your hand has guarded me! Be blessed,
And, if you like such reading, read, I pray,
Through Moses' book, or credit them who say
That old Isaiah's hand is far the best.

Some day, some day the potter shall return
Into the dust. O potter, will you make
An earth which I would not refuse to take,
Or such unpleasant earth as you would spurn?

Then out of that—men swear with godly skill—
Perchance another potter may devise
Another pot, a piece of merchandise
Which they can love and break, if so they will.

And from a resting-place you may be hurled
And from a score of countries may be thrust—
Poor brother, you the freeman of the dust,
Like any slave are flung about the world.

Made in the USA
Columbia, SC
12 July 2021